CHILDREN'S WORSHIP PROGRAM GUIDE

Each week we achieve our goal of reaching kids and their families for Christ by making programming for children Fun, Intentional, Scriptural, and Helpful.

FUN

The fun level of our activities should reflect the fun level of our God. 28nineteen™ KIDS teaches God's Word in a way that is attractive and memorable to the children. God is not boring, and neither are we! And, if children have a great time, they will want to return ... with friends!

INTENTIONAL

We are intentional about knowing these children's names and needs. God hand-picked the children who attend your church every weekend. They are precious to Him, and they are precious to us! The focus of 28nineteen™ KIDS is always on reaching children and their families for Jesus Christ.

SCRIPTURAL

28nineteen™ KIDS is an unapologetically Bible based curriculum. In other words, we stand on the Word of God. All of our Bible Study and Worship lessons come directly from the Bible and teach our children straight biblical truth.

HELPFUL

Our goal is to teach children to be "doers of the Word, and not merely hearers" (James 1:22). To do this, we teach practical applications of biblical truths in each lesson. The children should leave with a challenge or an action to live their lives for Christ.

TABLE OF CONTENTS

JUMP CHILDREN'S WORSHIP

JUMP is a worship service intentionally designed to teach elementary aged children the importance of worship. During JUMP, children express their worship through high-energy music and dancing. The Bible lesson is further enforced through fun, engaging skits and object lessons. You will discover that JUMP is an exciting and engaging curriculum for children's worship!

VIDEO ELEMENTS

High quality video elements are incorporated to capture each child's imagination and to allow time for transition between live elements.

SKIT

With every lesson, a fun skit is performed to help put the main point of the day into a humorous, modern and memorable scenario. These skits are fun and serve as object lessons for the Bible story and main point. You and your kids will love laughing and learning with these fun characters. Children will not want to miss a single lesson!

On the skit pages, screen elements and AUDIO ELEMENTS are highlighted as cues for your audio/visual team. Skits include a variety of descriptive sound effects; however, these are not included in the digital pack, as they are not absolutely necessary. You will need to obtain these online or make them yourselves.

Green text denotes important lines dealing with spiritual truths. Be sure your actors memorize the green lines!

MAIN POINT

The Bible is so rich! Every time we read a Bible story, be it the first or the fiftieth time, God can teach us something new. To help everyone stay on the same page, 28nineteen™ KIDS narrows in on one main point from the Bible story. Everything we do intentionally teaches the Bible story and this one point.

LEADER DEVOTION

The goal of the leader devotion is to help your leadership first learn the lesson personally which will help your leadership feel an empowerment and excitement to share what they have learned with their classes. For this reason, each lesson begins with the same devotion for all leaders on an adult level. Pertinent background information is incorporated to make the study richer in meaning for your leaders as well as for your kids.

JUMP BIBLE LESSON

JUMP Bible lessons are designed for large group teaching and often include object lessons and anecdotes to help teachers clearly present the Bible story and main point. Bible lessons are clearly outlined into three sections: Intro, Bible Story, and Application.

 Intro: Short for "introduction", this section helps leaders grab kids' attention, quickly review past lessons, teach the overarching theme of the series, and get kids excited about the Bible story.

 Read the Bible: Now we get to the good stuff! In this section, leaders encourage kids to read in the Bible as they discover God's Word for themselves.

 Object Lesson: Object lessons use everyday, ordinary objects to teach important spiritual truths. A good object lesson helps the audience remember the spiritual truth in a tangible way.

 Application: Our goal is to teach children to be "doers of the Word, and not merely hearers" (James 1:22). To do this, we teach practical applications of biblical truths in each lesson. The children should leave with a challenge or an action to live their lives for Christ.

JUMP TEAM

Often lessons refer to the JUMP Team. The JUMP Team is a group of highly committed, fun-loving volunteers. These upstanding high school volunteers and fun-loving adults lead worship by acting in skits, leading motions to songs, assisting with classroom management, interacting with children, and more.

ORDER OF SERVICE

Knowing each church has its own method of operating, JUMP curriculum is designed to be flexible. Each time segment in JUMP is clearly designated and can occur in whatever order you are most comfortable.

The following pages are an example of an order of service and are adaptable to any sized group.

JUMP CHILDREN'S WORSHIP
ORDER OF SERVICE

Pre-Service
This time before the service begins allows children to make it to their seats and interact with volunteers.

COUNTDOWN VIDEO

Song

MAIN POINT VIDEO

Welcome
The welcome is designed to introduce who is leading, what it means to worship, the rules for service, and what the children will learn that day. This should be done by the worship director, can involve a teacher/co-teacher scenario, and always ends with a prayer.

A few rules are said at the beginning of service so expectations for behavior are known. Always end with HAVE FUN!

Who's excited to be here today?! My name is (_____) and I am so happy you are here to worship with us! Today we are going to be learning that (MAIN POINT). Can you do those motions and say that with me on the count of three? One, two, three: (MAIN POINT). Oh, I think you can be louder than that! One, two, three: *(MAIN POINT)*. WOW! Great job!

As you know, we come to JUMP to worship God together. What are some ways we can worship the Lord? We can worship God by singing, dancing, reading our Bible, and even praying! These are all ways that we worship God together. We are going to do ALL of those things today! We are going to learn some AMAZING things about God's Word, so everyone please sit up straight, look up here at me, and turn on your listening ears!

We have a few rules to help us worship God together. Rule number one is: *(Stay quiet)*. When someone is speaking up here, please stay quiet. God has something to say to you and me today. We do not want to distract anyone from hearing exactly what the Lord has for us to hear.

Rule number two is: *(Keep your hands and feet to yourself)*. We worship God when we focus on Him alone and put Him first. Keeping your hands and feet to yourself will help you and everyone around you focus on God.

Rule number three is: *(Stand during songs)*. Anytime you hear a song, we stand so we can worship together, be reverent to the Lord, and show Him that we love Him. JUMP is a worship service, not a show. Stand up and participate with us when we worship through song!

Rule number four is: *(HAVE FUN)*! We are going to have so much fun today as we worship God together. Let's start this service right by talking to our amazing God in prayer right now.

PRAY

SKIT INTRO VIDEO

JUMP Skit Part 1
The skit falls before the JUMP Bible Lesson, so the pastor or teacher can refer back to the lessons the characters learned during the skit.

Song

BIBLE LESSON INTRO VIDEO

JUMP Bible Lesson

The Bible lesson falls roughly halfway through the service to make sure all of the kids have arrived. We do not want anyone to miss out on the best part! JUMP Bible lessons often include object lessons and anecdotes to help teachers clearly present the Bible story and main point in 15 minutes or less.

PRAY

We are about to go into our time of offering. "Offering" is a big word for present. This is the time when we give our presents to the Lord. We give back to God from everything He has given to us. Let's stand together and sing this song as an offering, a big present to God.

Offering Song

SKIT INTRO VIDEO

JUMP Skit Part 2

The resolution of the skit builds on the principles learned in the Bible lesson.

Song

MEMORY VERSE VIDEO

Memory Verse

The goal of the memory verse time is long-term understanding and memorization of Scripture. For this reason, 28nineteen Curriculum focuses on one verse or passage during each series. Throughout the series, kids are encouraged to memorize these verses by making motions to the words and repeating the verse together.

Song

Announcements

What can the children look forward to in your ministry? Use this time to encourage kids to bring friends and participate in whatever you may have coming up next.

Review Game

Play a fun game that allows everyone to remember what they have learned.

It's time for the REVIEW GAME! I need one volunteer from each grade to come up on stage. I want to choose people who have been listening and paying attention the whole service and want to play in our game!

During this game, your grade can win by getting very quiet when you hear the wrong answer and very loud when you hear the right answer. Each grade is going to have a different silly move and sound that you must do when you think you hear the right answer. (Let your contestants choose a silly motion and sound for their grade.)

I hope you are ready. I hope you have been paying attention. The game begins ... NOW!

(Ask review questions. Give kids the opportunity to do their motions and silly sounds when they hear the correct answer. Award points to the winning grade.)

Song

Dismissal

STATION
OVERVIEW

OVERARCHING PLOT

Welcome to JUMP NEWS with your news team: Weather with Wendy Storm, Traffic with Iona Ford, Sports with Will Wynn, Politics with Cam Pain, and news anchors, Justin Report and Johnny Onthespot. Due to a clerical error, the entire established news team has gone on vacation at the same time. Interns Jamie Jamison and Scoop Blakely have to step in and report the news to viewers like you.

CHARACTERS

JAMIE JAMISON – former intern who becomes a serious reporter

SCOOP BLAKELY – former intern in charge of coffee who becomes a goofy news reporter

PRODUCER – in charge of running the show, commercial breaks, etc.

COSTUMES

JAMIE JAMISON – "JUMP News" jumpsuit with slacks, button-down shirt, and tie underneath

SCOOP BLAKELY – "JUMP News" jumpsuit with slacks, button-down shirt, and tie underneath

PRODUCER – All black clothing with headsset and clipboard

SET

JUMP News Room - News desk, Two chairs, Camera

LESSON 1

BIBLE LESSON

THE WISE AND FOOLISH BUILDERS
Luke 6:46-49

MAIN POINT

WISE PEOPLE BUILD THEIR LIVES ON JESUS.

MEMORY VERSE

LUKE 4:18-19 "The Spirit of the Lord is upon me, for he has anointed me to bring Good News to the poor. He has sent me to proclaim that captives will be released, that the blind will see, that the oppressed will be set free, and that the time of the Lord's favor has come."

LESSON 1
HIGHLIGHTS

SPIRITUAL CONNECTION

Jamie and Scoop report on a building competition that mirrors the parable of the wise and foolish builders in Luke 6. When a big storm comes, the fancy house with a sandy foundation collapses, but the simple house with a good foundation stands firm. A good foundation is important in building and in life.

CHARACTERS

JAMIE JAMISON – former intern who becomes a serious reporter

SCOOP BLAKELY – former intern in charge of coffee who becomes a goofy news reporter

PRODUCER – in charge of running the show, commercial breaks, etc.

COSTUMES

JAMIE JAMISON – "JUMP News" jumpsuit with slacks, button-down shirt, and tie underneath

SCOOP BLAKELY – "JUMP News" jumpsuit with slacks, button-down shirt, and tie underneath

PRODUCER – All black clothing with headset and clipboard

SET

JUMP News Room - News desk, Two chairs, Camera

Construction Zone - Yellow tape, Traffic cones, Ladders, Tool chests, Wood planks, etc.

PROPS

Skit - Cue cards, Clipboard, Coffee cups, Papers/pencils for desk, Microphone, Wood planks and other various building supplies, Bowling pin

Lesson - 1 Large, sturdy, rectangular box, 3 Medium boxes (to fit on top of the larger box), 2 Small boxes (to fit on top of the medium boxes), 1 Tiny box (to fit on top of the small boxes), Thick marker

JUMP NEWS

LEADER DEVOTION

READ   LUKE 6:46-49

"So why do you keep calling me 'Lord, Lord!' when you don't do what I say?" Luke 6:46

This is one of the most convicting questions Jesus asks His followers. In Luke 6, Jesus ends His sermon with this parable, reminding the disciples of the benefits in implementing His teachings and the folly of only listening. Interestingly, there are only two builders in the parable, indicating two choices in life: the choice to obey Christ and the choice to ignore Him. There is no builder who constructs half of his house on rock and the other half without a foundation. Indecision is not an option.

The wise builder laid a foundation on the rock, because he considered the long-term effects of his construction choices. He built a house that would last through any storm. The foolish builder, however, may have built without a foundation for any number of reasons: ignorance of possible storms, location, view, time constraints, financial concerns, etc. Picture the two houses in your mind. Do they look the same? For some reason, I imagine the house on the rock as a simple, practical house and the house without a foundation as an extravagant mansion. I imagine the foolish builder unwisely used his money to make his home more luxurious than sturdy. He focused on the short-term benefits of his construction choices.

God is often referred to in the Old Testament as the only Rock, the only Foundation who cannot be moved (1 Samuel 2:2; 2 Samuel 22:47; Psalm 62:2). Jesus is the Rock, because He is God. He will not change with the times. **Hebrews 13:8 says, "Jesus Christ is the same yesterday, today, and forever."** Building our lives to be completely dependent on Christ ensures eternal victory through every storm life throws our way.

What is the foundation of your life? Is Christ so centrally important to your life that nothing would function without Him? If your answer is no, allow the Lord to completely wreck your life, so that you can rebuild on Him, the One who never fails. We must trust our Rock completely, building everything we are in this life on Him. Take time this week to thank God for being your firm Foundation throughout your life. Thank Him for His commands and ask Him to help you do what He says every day of your life.

PRE-SERVICE

Play fun music and videos as kids come into JUMP Worship. Skit characters Jamie and Scoop hold up various cue cards ("Applause," "Laugh," "Oooh," "Ahhh," "Oh no," etc.) during the music and videos, encouraging kids to participate.

COUNTDOWN VIDEO

JUMP Worship is starting! Lead the congregation in counting down. Worshiping together is fun, and we are ready to begin!

SONG

Lead the congregation in a fun worship song.

MAIN POINT VIDEO

WELCOME

Welcome to JUMP, where we worship God together! As you can see, we are in a newsroom for our new series, JUMP News. For the next few weeks, we are going to learn about Jesus from book of Luke. We hear a lot of news stories every day, but in JUMP News we are learning about the greatest news of all time. Jesus is the best news the world has ever received! We should all tell the world about Jesus.

Our Main Point is "Wise People Build Their Lives on Jesus." Each piece of our lives is important, but nothing should be more important to us than Jesus! *(Make motions for the Main Point. Have kids repeat the motions and Main Point with you.)*

Now turn to your neighbor and say, "Hello!" (*Hello!*)
Turn to your other neighbor and say, "What's up?" (*What's up?*)
Tell them your name. Introduce yourself. (*Kids introduce themselves.*)
Now say "Listen!" (*Listen!*)
"Wise people build their lives on Jesus!" (*Wise people build their lives on Jesus!*)
Turn to the person behind you and say, "Hey, back of your head!" (*Hey, back of your head!*)
"Wise people build their lives on Jesus!" (*Wise people build their lives on Jesus!*)
Face me and say one last time, "Wise people build their lives on Jesus!" (*Wise people build their lives on Jesus!*)

Great job! I can't wait to open the Bible and learn more about this with all of you as we worship today. We have a few rules to help us worship God, to keep our focus on Him and Him alone. Rule number one is STAY QUIET. When someone is up here talking, we should all be listening. Show me what that should look and sound like. (*Wait for kids to be quiet.*) Great job! Listening will help us stay focused on God.

Our second rule is KEEP YOUR HANDS AND FEET TO YOURSELF. Focusing on God is very difficult when the people around you are messing with you. Don't distract the people around you from worshiping God! Keep your hands and feet to yourself.

Rule number three is STAND UP DURING SONGS. JUMP is not a show. We are here to worship God together, so be a part of what we are doing. Think about the words of the songs when you sing. Use your hands and feet to worship God, not to mess with your friends.

And finally, our fourth rule is – say it with me – HAVE FUN! We are going to have so much fun today! Now let's worship God by talking to Him in prayer. Bow your heads and close your eyes. Focus on God only as we talk to Him.

PRAY

Lead the congregation in prayer.

JUMP SKIT PART 1

See skit script beginning on page 14.

LESSON 1 SKIT
PART 1

THE WISE AND FOOLISH BUILDERS

WISE PEOPLE BUILD THEIR LIVES ON JESUS.

Skit Intro Video

Welcome to JUMP NEWS with your news team: Weather with Wendy Storm, Traffic with Iona Ford, Sports with Will Wynn, Politics with Cam Pain, and news anchors, Justin Report and Johnny Onthespot.

SFX: NEWS TRANSITION MUSIC

Lights up, but no one appears.

SFX: NEWS TRANSITION MUSIC

Producer enters.

PRODUCER: Due to a clerical error, all our news team has gone on vacation at the same time ...

Producer holds up cue card that says, "Oh No!"

PRODUCER: So, we've followed news protocol to determine the replacement news team. Oh yes. Our first replacement news anchor is news intern ... *Scans clipboard.* Jamie Jamison!

JAMIE: Oh, what?! I've never done this! I'm so nervous, I wasn't expecting this ... *Flips voice into news anchor voice and unzips his jumpsuit to reveal a news anchor suit.* Welcome to JUMP NEWS. I'm your anchor, Jamie Jamison. Here to bring you the latest-breaking news that will pull at your heart strings and make your mind go, "Wow! That's some interesting news." And remember, you heard it here first with Jamie Jamison. When life gives you lemons, check for mold.

PRODUCER: And your co-anchor will be ... *Looks at clipboard.* Scoop Blakely.

Producer holds up "Applause" sign, but no one enters the stage.

PRODUCER: Scoop? Is there a Scoop Blakely here? Anyone know a Scoop?

Scoop runs on in a panic with multiple coffee cups.

SCOOP: I'm so sorry! I'm here! I was just getting all the news anchors' coffees. They told me that they needed specific coffee orders and if I messed them up ... I'm just an intern. I'm sorry I was late.

PRODUCER: Are you Scoop Blakely?

SCOOP: I'm so sorry! This is all my fault. This is on me! I took a turn too fast, and I spilled the coffee.

PRODUCER: Scoop, calm down.

SCOOP: She wanted the pink package, not the yellow. And he wanted a venti, not a grande. And what is chai?!?!?

PRODUCER: Scoop, you have been selected as the second replacement news anchor.

SCOOP: What? Me? Are you serious? *High scream and gasp. Runs around excited!* Oh, I've got to sit down. *Changes voice.* Okay. Must prepare. What are we talking about today? Need some time for warm-ups. *Tries out different versions.* I'm SCOOP Blakely. I'm Scoop BLAKEly. Hello, Scoop Blakely here. Ugh. I don't know if I can do this!

PRODUCER: And we're live in 3, 2, 1 ...

SCOOP: What? *Goes big eyed and freezes.*

JAMIE: Welcome to JUMP NEWS. I'm your anchor, Jamie Jamison, here to bring you the latest breaking news with my co-anchor ...

SCOOP: *Wide eyed and shocked, finally quietly speaks.* ... Scoop -

JAMIE: *Whispering.* Louder!

SCOOP: *Yells.* SCOOP!

PRODUCER: Go to commercial!

Video: Commercial

PRODUCER: Come on, Scoop, I need you to pick it up. This is live television. Pull yourself together! And we're live in 3, 2, 1 ....

JAMIE: Welcome back to JUMP NEWS. I'm your anchor, Jamie Jamison, here to bring you the latest breaking news that will pull at your heart strings and make your mind go, "Wow! That's some interesting news."

SCOOP: *Yelling.* WE'RE BACK! I AM SCOOP. HERE TO GIVE YOU THE SCOOP.

JAMIE: Thank you, Scoop. Nice intro, by the way. Alright, now we're going to go live in the field to bring you this breaking story… SFX: BREAKING NEWS STORY *Holds finger to ear.* Oh wait, what is that? I'm getting word that all our field reporters are on vacation, too. Scoop, we need you to go out into the field to cover this story.

SCOOP: What?! I'll never get there in time! This is live television!

JAMIE: Extreme Home Makeover Builders and Contractors is having a competition, and you have to be the judge. We need you to get out to the site as fast as you can. Word on the street is there could be a massive storm heading toward them. You can do this, Scoop. Just remember, when life gives you lemons, check for mold. Now get out there!

SCOOP: What does that even mean?!

JAMIE: Go!

Scoop exits frantically.

JAMIE: We'll be right back with more JUMP NEWS. I'm Jamie Jamison.

SFX: NEWS TRANSITION MUSIC

Jamie exits.

SONG *Lead the congregation in a fun worship song.*

SPECIAL REPORT
FROM THE BIBLE

JUMP NEWS

BIBLE LESSON INTRO VIDEO

 OBJECT LESSON

Who here has ever built a real house? No one? Okay, who here has ever built a tower out of blocks? Lots of you! Great! I'm going to build a tower using giant blocks, so everyone can see. I don't build a lot of towers, so I might mess this up a few times. Just bear with me while I figure this out!

Try to build the tower with the smallest box on the bottom and the largest box on the top. Make a big show of all the blocks falling over. Try to build the tower this way several times, until the kids start yelling out the correct way to build the tower.

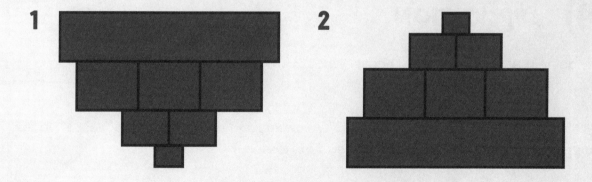

Then build the tower with the biggest box on the bottom and the smallest box on the top.

Building that tower was a bit harder than I thought it would be, because I started to build with the wrong box. Can you imagine if someone tried to build a house that way? The bottom of the house is called the foundation. The foundation needs to be the strongest part of the house, because everything else in the house sits on top of the foundation. If the foundation is not strong, the house will not stand for very long.

INTRO

This week, we are starting our new series on the book of Luke. The book of Luke tells us about Jesus, as told by people who actually saw Jesus when He lived on earth. Luke is one of four eye-witness accounts in the Bible of what happened when Jesus was living on the earth.

Luke chapter 6 tells us Jesus was teaching the people about God. When He finished, Jesus told a parable about two houses. A parable is a made-up story that helps us understand big truths. This parable is called "The Wise and Foolish Builders."

READ THE BIBLE

Read Luke 6:46-49.

One builder built his house on a rock. That is a very good foundation! The other builder decided he did not need a foundation. He did not think a good foundation was important. When the storms came, the house with no foundation collapsed, but the house with a foundation stood strong.

APPLICATION

Imagine that your life is like a house. What would the different rooms be? Sports? Music? School? Family?

Write these "room" names on the medium, small, and tiny boxes. Write "Jesus" on the biggest box. Use these boxes as you end the lesson.

All of the pieces of our lives are important to us, but there is only one thing that is worthy of being our solid foundation - Jesus! Your relationship with Jesus should affect every "room" in your life. If Jesus is your Foundation, the way you play sports should be different from someone who does not know Jesus. If Jesus is your Foundation, your words will be based on your relationship with Jesus. If Jesus is our Foundation, you and I will not only hear what Jesus says in the Bible, but we will also do what Jesus tells us to do in the Bible. We will begin to put Jesus' words into action, as we get to know Him more and more each day.

Then when the storms of life come (losing the big game, parents fighting, moving to a new school, friends asking you to do something you know is wrong, etc.), you will be able to stand for the Lord. You will know Jesus loves you and is with you no matter what happens, no matter what anyone else says. You will know your life is not falling apart, because Jesus is the One who is holding you together. Wise people build their lives on Jesus.

PRAY

OFFERING SONG

Lead the congregation in a slower worship song.

JUMP SKIT PART 2

See skit script beginning on page 20.

WISE PEOPLE BUILD THEIR LIVES ON JESUS.

JUMP NEWS

LESSON 1 SKIT
PART 2

THE WISE AND FOOLISH BUILDERS

WISE PEOPLE BUILD THEIR LIVES ON JESUS.

Skit Intro Video

Welcome to JUMP NEWS with your news team: Weather with Wendy Storm, Traffic with Iona Ford, Sports with Will Wynn, Politics with Cam Pain, and news anchors, Justin Report and Johnny Onthespot.

SFX: NEWS TRANSITION MUSIC

JAMIE: Welcome back to JUMP NEWS, I'm Jamie Jamison. Here to bring you the latest-breaking news that will pull at your heart strings and make your mind go, "Wow! That's some interesting news."

Producer holds up "Applause" sign.

JAMIE: We have Scoop Blakely live in the field with this fascinating story. What's the scoop, Scoop?

Lights up on the Construction Zone. Scoop gets interrupted by workers walking by with construction materials.

SCOOP: That's right, Jamie. I'm out here with some friendly competitors - Extreme Home Makeover Builders and Contractors. **SFX: CONSTRUCTION** Team One seems to be building their house on a solid foundation. Looks like it's maybe made of rock? BORING.

But check it out! Team Two appears to have skipped the whole "rock" thing and is building on the cool stuff! They're building their house on pure sand! GENIUS! And look, they've installed a pool and a bowling alley and a fire pole which leads into a giant pool of Jell-O!

Jamie, I really think there's no competition amongst these competitors. Clearly, Team Two has the coolest house! Back to you in the studio!

JAMIE: Scoop, thank you for that report. But are you sure it was a good idea to skip building on a solid foundation? For a house to stand steadily, it needs to be built on something solid. The pool and Jell-O sound fun and all, but I'm not sure that Team Two is going to win.

SCOOP: It looks like Team Two isn't just using ordinary "beach" sand ... this sand has been packed down and saturated with water. This should last, most definitely, for centuries to come.

JAMIE: *Holds finger up to ear.* Oh wait, hold on. Sorry to interrupt you, Scoop, but I'm getting news that a torrential thunderstorm is headed your way.

Producer holds up "Oh No!" sign.

SCOOP: Awesome! I'm going to ride out this storm in the bowling alley! Hey-o!

JAMIE: I really think you should go to a safer place, Scoop. Maybe take cover in Team One's house. This looks to be a really big storm.

SCOOP: But Team One's house doesn't have a pool of Jell-O.

Lights flicker.

SFX: LIGHTNING

JAMIE: Yes, but it is built on a solid foundation.

SCOOP: Alright, the storm is coming ... I'm headed to Team Two's house! I'm going to go bowling and roll four chickens!

JAMIE: I think they're called turkeys, Scoop.

SCOOP: Strike!

Lights down.

SFX: STORM

JAMIE: This just in: the storm has officially passed. The storm tore through this neighborhood. Homeowners are now reappearing on the streets to check the status of their homes.

Scoop drags himself back onstage and is disheveled.

SCOOP: I'm here. That storm was very, very fast and very devastating. All. I have. Left. Is This. One. Bowling Pin. The rest of Team Two's house is completely gone.

JAMIE: How is Team One's house holding up?

SCOOP: It appears you were right. They are safe and sound inside.
Producer holds up "Applause" sign.

SCOOP: They appear to be drinking hot chocolate and watching a movie about an orange and white fish that is lost. I feel a lot like that fish right now. Back to you, Jamie.

JAMIE: You know Scoop, this reminds me of the special report we heard today about the wise and foolish builders. The wise men built their house on the rock, and we have to remember to build our lives on a firm foundation, too.

SCOOP: Yeah, you're right.

JAMIE: Thank you for that update. I think it's pretty clear that Team One won this competition. See what I did there, Team One – won?! I'm a natural at this. The team that built its house on the rock, the solid foundation, was much smarter than the builders who built their house on the sand. This has been JUMP NEWS with Jamie Jamison and Scoop Blakely. And remember, when life gives you lemons, check for mold.

SFX: NEWS TRANSITION MUSIC

Video: Commercial

SONG *Lead the congregation in a fun worship song.*

MEMORY VERSE VIDEO

MEMORY VERSE

Our memory verse is from the book of Luke, chapter four, verses eighteen and nineteen. In these verses, Jesus is reading from the book of Isaiah. These verses are about Jesus!

Read the verses with me. **Luke 4:18-19 "The Spirit of the LORD is upon me, for he has anointed me to bring Good News to the poor. He has sent me to proclaim that captives will be released, that the blind will see, that the oppressed will be set free, and that the time of the LORD's favor has come."**

The Good News is that Jesus made a way for us to have a right relationship with God. Jesus is the best news the world has ever received! Let's make motions to the first part of this verse.

(Make motions for the key words and phrases in the first sentence of the verse. Use these motions each time you say the verse.)

Repeat after me.
Luke 4:18-19 *(Luke 4:18-19)*
"The Spirit of the LORD *(The Spirit of the LORD)*
is upon me *(is upon me)*,
for he has anointed me *(for he has anointed me)*
to bring Good News *(to bring Good News)*
to the poor *(to the poor)*."

Now let's say this part of the verse all together, starting with "Luke 4:18-19" on the count of three. One, two, three: **Luke 4:18-19 "The Spirit of the LORD is upon me, for he has anointed me to bring Good News to the poor."**

Great job! Jesus is the best news the world has ever received. I challenge you to tell someone the Good News about Jesus this week.

ANNOUNCEMENTS

Use this time to encourage kids to bring friends and participate in whatever you may have coming up next.

REVIEW GAME

It's time for the REVIEW GAME!! I need one volunteer from each grade to come up on stage. I will choose people who have been listening and paying attention the whole service and want to play in our game.

Choose contestants and introduce them to the group in game show style.

During this game, your grade can win by getting very quiet when you hear the wrong answer and very loud when you hear the right answer. Each grade is going to have a different silly move and sound that you must do when you think you hear the right answer. *(Let your contestants choose a silly motion and sound for their grade.)*

I hope you are ready. I hope you have been paying attention, because the game begins ... NOW!

Give kids the opportunity to do their motions and silly sounds when they hear the correct answer. Award points to the grade who is the quietest when they hear the wrong answer and participates the most when they hear the right answer.

Question 1: What was today's Main Point?
    a. Wise People Are Old.   c. Foolish People Go to the Beach.
    b. Wise People Build Their   d. Wise People Build Houses.
    Lives on Jesus.

Question 2: Where can you find today's Bible lesson?
    a. Luke 6:46–49   c. Leviticus 6:46–49
    b. Matthew 6:46–49   d. Mark 6:46–49

Question 3: What was the foolish man's foundation?
    a. Pools of Gelatin   **c. Sand**
    b. Rock   d. Rubber ducks

Question 4: What happened to the foolish man when the storm came?
    a. His house stood firm.   c. His dog ran away.
    b. His house collapsed.   d. His cat scratched his face.

Question 5: Who should be the center of our lives, our foundation?
    a. Me, Myself, and I   c. My family
    b. My friends   **d. Jesus**

Question 6: Luke 4:18a says, "The Spirit of the LORD is upon me, for he has anointed me to bring _____ to the poor."

    a. Good Apple Juice   **c. Good News**

    b. Good Money   d. Nachos

SONG

Lead the congregation in a fun worship song.

DISMISSAL

"THE SPIRIT OF THE LORD IS UPON ME, FOR HE HAS ANOINTED ME TO BRING GOOD NEWS TO THE POOR. HE HAS SENT ME TO PROCLAIM THAT CAPTIVES WILL BE RELEASED, THAT THE BLIND WILL SEE, THAT THE OPPRESSED WILL BE SET FREE, AND THAT THE TIME OF THE LORD'S FAVOR HAS COME."

LUKE 4:18-19

REPORTING
LIVE
FROM THE
BOOK OF LUKE

LESSON 2

BIBLE LESSON

JESUS ANOINTED BY A SINFUL WOMAN
Luke 7:36-50

MAIN POINT

JESUS LOVES ME, SO I CAN LOVE OTHERS.

MEMORY VERSE

LUKE 4:18-19 "The Spirit of the Lord is upon me, for he has anointed me to bring Good News to the poor. He has sent me to proclaim that captives will be released, that the blind will see, that the oppressed will be set free, and that the time of the Lord's favor has come."

LESSON 2
HIGHLIGHTS

SPIRITUAL CONNECTION

Jamie and Scoop report on a red carpet event that closely mirrors the events in Luke 7:36-50. When a little boy approaches the famous celebrity, Joshua Reyes, other celebrities look down on him for talking to the boy. Reyes says he believes all people should be treated with equal love and care, regardless of what anyone else thinks.

CHARACTERS

JAMIE JAMISON – former intern who becomes a serious reporter

SCOOP BLAKELY – former intern in charge of coffee who becomes a goofy news reporter

PRODUCER – in charge of running the show, commercial breaks, etc.

JOSHUA REYES – famous rapper/singer/actor

VARIOUS CELEBRITIES – pass by Scoop on the red carpet, point and laugh at Joshua Reyes

LITTLE BOY – fan of Joshua Reyes

COSTUMES

JAMIE JAMISON – Slacks, Button-down shirt, Tie

SCOOP BLAKELY – Slacks, Button-down shirt, Tie

PRODUCER – All black clothing with headset and clipboard

JOSHUA REYES – Street clothes and sunglasses

VARIOUS CELEBRITIES – Glamourous clothing

LITTLE BOY – Everyday attire

SET

JUMP News Room – News desk, Two chairs, Camera

Red Carpet Event – Red carpet, Movie themed decorations, etc.

PROPS

Skit - Cue cards, Clipboard, Coffee cups, Papers/pencils for desk, Microphone, Red carpet

Lesson - Gallon jug of water with "Jesus" label, Cup with a hole in the bottom and "Me" label, Several different cups, Paper towels

JUMP NEWS

LEADER DEVOTION

After reading this passage, you can't help feeling sorry for the Pharisee who is missing out on all that Jesus has to offer him. The woman chose to receive Jesus' grace and mercy in full, and it overwhelmed her with gratitude. She had to do something to show her thanks and devotion to her Savior. Simon, though, did not participate in worship. He missed out on the miracle of forgiveness and the realization of who Jesus really was, because he was so preoccupied with his pride and judgments.

The Pharisee's pride would not allow him to see beyond the woman's sinful past to understand the beautiful act of worship she gave to Jesus. Jesus, however, saw the woman as He created her. He received her worship with love and forgiveness, coming to her defense before Simon even spoke a word of judgment.

Do you have a past that haunts you? Do you sometimes feel the judgmental looks of the "righteous" who knew of you before you met Jesus? Christian, never forget you have been forgiven by the Son of God, who made you and loves you. You have accepted Jesus' forgiveness, once and for all, and now live in the confidence you have a Redeemer who will defend you. Christ is your Redeemer, not the self-righteous. Worship the Lord without fear!

Or perhaps you have been the judgmental Pharisee. Simon, like many of the Pharisees in Jesus' time, considered himself to be self-sufficient and righteous by his own power. Because he considered his need for the Savior to be small, he had little capacity to love and embrace the Savior when face-to-face with the Son of God.

Jesus' parable in verses 40-43 is not to encourage us to sin more, so we can love Him more. Instead, it is to encourage us to mourn over our sins, so we can understand our need for Him. It is to encourage us to judge less and love more, to see ourselves and others as God sees us. We all owe a debt we cannot pay. We all stand before the throne of God in desperate need of forgiveness. And thanks to Jesus, we all have a Savior who has paid our debt in full, who stands in defense of those who choose to wholeheartedly love Him. What other response can there be but worship?

PRE-SERVICE

Play fun music and videos as kids come into JUMP Worship. Skit characters Jamie and Scoop hold up various cue cards ("Applause," "Laugh," "Oooh," "Ahhh," "Oh no," etc.) during the music and videos, encouraging kids to participate.

COUNTDOWN VIDEO

JUMP Worship is starting! Lead the congregation in counting down. Worshiping together is fun, and we are ready to begin!

SONG

Lead the congregation in a fun worship song.

MAIN POINT VIDEO

WELCOME

Welcome to JUMP, where we worship God together! Does anyone remember what book of the Bible we are studying during our series, JUMP News? *(Luke)* Yes! Great job! We are studying Luke's collection of eye-witness accounts of Jesus' time on earth. We hear a lot of news stories every day, but in JUMP News we are learning about the greatest news of all time. Jesus is the best news the world has ever received! We should all tell the world about Jesus.

Our Main Point is "Jesus Loves Me, So I Can Love Others." Jesus loves each and every person here. We do not have to worry about trying to be better than anyone else. Jesus already loves us! I want to love people the way Jesus does. Let's make motions to help us remember our Main Point. *(Make motions for the Main Point. Have kids repeat the motions and Main Point with you.)*

Now turn to your neighbor and say, "Hello!" (*Hello!*)

Turn to your other neighbor and say, "What's up?" (*What's up?*)

Tell them your name. Introduce yourself. (*Kids introduce themselves.*)

Now say "Hey!" (*Hey!*)

"Jesus Loves Me, So I Can Love Others." (*Jesus Loves Me, So I Can Love Others.*)

Point to (*name a volunteer*) and say, "You are amazing!" (*You are amazing!*)

"Jesus loves you!" (*Jesus loves you!*)

"And Jesus loves me, so I can love others!" (*And Jesus loves me, so I can love others!*)

Face me and say one last time, "Jesus Loves Me, So I Can Love Others." (*Jesus Loves Me, So I Can Love Others.*)

Great job! I can't wait to open the Bible and learn more about this as we worship today. We have a few rules to help us worship God, to keep our focus on Him and Him alone. Rule number one is STAY QUIET. When someone is up here talking, we should all be listening. Show me what that should look and sound like. (*Wait for kids to be quiet.*) Great job! Listening will help us stay focused on God.

Our second rule is KEEP YOUR HANDS AND FEET TO YOURSELF. Focusing on God is very difficult when the people around you are messing with you. Don't distract the people around you from worshiping God! Keep your hands and feet to yourself.

Rule number three is STAND UP DURING SONGS. JUMP is not a show. We are here to worship God together, so be a part of what we are doing. Think about the words of the songs when you sing. Use your hands and feet to worship God, not to mess with your friends.

And finally, our fourth rule is – say it with me – HAVE FUN! We are going to have so much fun today! Now let's worship God by talking to Him in prayer. Bow your heads and close your eyes. Focus on God only as we talk to Him.

PRAY

Lead the congregation in prayer.

JUMP SKIT PART 1

See skit script beginning on page 32.

LESSON 2 SKIT
PART 1

JESUS ANOINTED BY A SINFUL WOMAN

JESUS LOVES ME, SO I CAN LOVE OTHERS.

Skit Intro Video

Welcome to JUMP NEWS with your news team: Weather with Wendy Storm, Traffic with Iona Ford, Sports with Will Wynn, Politics with Cam Pain, and news anchors, Justin Report and Johnny Onthespot.

SFX: NEWS TRANSITION MUSIC

JAMIE: Welcome back to JUMP NEWS! I'm Jamie Jamison, your JUMP NEWS reporter. Here to bring you the latest-breaking news that will pull at your heart strings and make your mind go, "Wow! That's some interesting news."

Producer holds up "Applause" sign.

JAMIE: I might be a temporary news reporter while all the other anchors are on vacation, but I've always been a news reporter at heart. And my co-anchor should be joining me at any moment ... *Looks around for him.*

Scoop runs on with multiple coffees and sits at the desk.

SCOOP: AND WE'RE BACK! No worries, I got everyone's coffee order. This one's for Scoop. Who's Scoop? Oh, I'm Scoop! *Takes a drink and spits it out.* Yowza! This is disgusting. This must be yesterday's coffee.

JAMIE: All the people you got coffee for are on vacation. Remember? And if that's yesterday's coffee, then why were you late?

SCOOP: *Suddenly bright eyed and scared.* Ummmmm I'M SCOOP, HERE TO BRING YOU THE LATEST SCOOP!

JAMIE: Thank you, Scoop. Now for breaking news. **SFX: BREAKING NEWS** This just in. A man is stuck in a tree, and a rescue cat is there now trying to retrieve the man. Oh wait, no - there is a cat stuck in a tree and a man trying to rescue him. Ah, now that makes a lot more sense! Hahaha!

SCOOP: You cat to be kitten me right meow. See what I did there?

Producer holds up "Laugh" sign.

JAMIE: *Puts hand to ear.* Wait, what's this? More breaking news? WHAT A DAY THIS IS! It appears that Commander Cobalt just arrived on the scene and is attempting to rescue the cat. But what's this? The famous superhero, Spark, has just flown to rescue the cat and Commander Cobalt from the tree! Well done, team! What do you think about all this, Scoop?

Scoop doesn't reply.

JAMIE: Scoop? Did you hear me? What do you think? Are you okay?

SCOOP: What do you mean? I just told that whole story about the cat and Spark and Commander Cobalt!

JAMIE: No, you didn't. I told that story.

SCOOP: Oh, you're right. That wasn't me. *Nervous laughter. He grabs the "Laugh" sign from the Producer and holds it up.* I think I must be having some stage fright. I'm feeling nervous. My eyebrows are sweating, and my nose is starting to twitch, and my foot is starting to bounce and...

JAMIE: Woah, there, Scoop. Hold it together. *Aside.* You are live on the air! Don't look at me! Look at the camera! *Back to the camera.* Incredible! MORE BREAKING NEWS! SFX: BREAKING NEWS   This just in. There is a red carpet event on the corner of Main and 5th! There are more celebrities than we can count. But you, our viewers, will get to feel like you're a part of the red carpet event, because we, JUMP NEWS, are going to bring it all to you LIVE right here! What is this? The field reporters are still on vacation? Scoop, get out there!

SCOOP: What? Oh! AND WE'RE BACK!!

JAMIE: No, Scoop!

SCOOP: We're not back!

JAMIE: We need you out in the field, reporting live from the corner of Main and 5th Street!

SCOOP: Right. Scoop Blakely, reporting live.

JAMIE: Scoop!! Get out in the field!

SCOOP: Got it! I'm on it!

SFX: NEWS TRANSITION MUSIC

Jamie and Scoop exit in opposite directions.

SONG *Lead the congregation in a fun worship song.*

SPECIAL REPORT
FROM THE BIBLE

JUMP NEWS

BIBLE LESSON INTRO VIDEO

 INTRO

Have any of you ever been embarrassed? Maybe you tripped, and everyone was looking?

Tell an appropriate embarrassing story.

Feeling embarrassed is no fun! Most of the time, we are able to laugh about the embarrassing moment later. In that moment, though, being embarrassed feels awful! No one likes people to look down on them. Unfortunately, in today's Bible story, a woman was looked down on by everyone around her - except for Jesus. Jesus honored the woman when everyone else was judging her.

 READ THE BIBLE

Read Luke 7:36-38.

Awkward! Jesus was having dinner at Simon the Pharisee's house when this woman invited herself in. She started pouring expensive perfume all over Jesus' feet and wiping His feet with her tears. What was going on here?

In Bible times, it was customary for a servant to wash everyone's feet before eating a meal. People greeted each other with a kiss and often anointed their guests' heads with oil. When Jesus came to the Pharisee's house, the only person to welcome Him was this woman - and it wasn't even her house!

Walking into someone else's house to give a beautiful present like that to Jesus must have taken a lot of courage. After all, what would people think when they saw her?

What if they knew about her past mistakes?

Read Luke 7:39.

Apparently, Simon the Pharisee did know about her past mistakes. He knew she had sinned. Everyone in the town knew this woman had made a lot of wrong choices in her life.

Simon chose to look down on the woman, because he did not understand what she was doing. The woman was worshiping Jesus. She was giving Jesus a present from her heart to thank Him for loving her, for forgiving her for her past sins. Jesus, the only One who had never sinned, did not look down on the woman. In fact, Jesus stood up for her!

Read Luke 7:44-48.

Simon the Pharisee did not understand that he needed Jesus' love and forgiveness just as much as the woman did. Unfortunately, Simon missed how incredible it was that Jesus was at HIS house! Simon did not appreciate Jesus. But because the woman really understood who Jesus was, she could not help but show Him love. She could not help but worship Him with all that she had - no matter what anyone else thought about her.

APPLICATION

Our main point today is "Jesus loves me, so I can love others." Simon did not understand God's love, so he did not show love to the woman. He judged her instead and missed out on an opportunity to worship Jesus. The woman, though, understood Jesus' love. She couldn't help showering God's love on everyone around her! No one could stop her from worshiping Jesus!

OBJECT LESSON

It's kind of like these cups. This big water jug represents Jesus' love. In real life, Jesus' love NEVER runs out, but it is too hard for me to hold more than one gallon. You'll have to use your imagination! Pretend this big gallon jug is a never ending supply of water.

This cup represents you and me. We were all designed to be filled up with God's love. Notice there is a hole in the bottom of the cup. God's love is never ending. We are supposed to receive God's love, then let is overflow onto everyone we meet!

Pour the water through the cup with the hole into the other cups.
So what does that mean in real life? You and I don't have to worry what anyone else thinks. We already know that the God of the Universe knows us and loves us very much! We all need Jesus' love. Jesus loves us all the same, so we should love everyone the same as well. Don't be like Simon, constantly judging other people. Instead, understand that Jesus' love has made you free to love others the way God loves you.

PRAY

OFFERING SONG

Lead the congregation in a slower worship song.

JUMP SKIT PART 2

See skit script beginning on page 38.

JESUS LOVES ME,
SO I CAN
LOVE OTHERS.

JUMP NEWS

LESSON 2 SKIT
PART 2

JESUS ANOINTED BY A SINFUL WOMAN

JESUS LOVES ME, SO I CAN LOVE OTHERS.

Skit Intro Video

Welcome to JUMP NEWS with your news team: Weather with Wendy Storm, Traffic with Iona Ford, Sports with Will Wynn, Politics with Cam Pain, and news anchors, Justin Report and Johnny Onthespot.

SFX: NEWS TRANSITION MUSIC

JAMIE: We're back with JUMP NEWS, I'm Jamie Jamison.

Producer holds up "Applause" sign.

JAMIE: We're excited to bring you an exclusive interview at the red carpet event happening right now. Give us the scoop, Scoop!

Lights up on Scoop standing next to a red carpet.

SCOOP: This is Scoop Blakely, reporting live from the corner of Main and 5th Street at the red carpet event of the century.

JAMIE: Tell us, Scoop, who do you see? Who's there?

SCOOP: Well, let's see … There's a man with sunglasses and little tiny ear buds. I think his name is Joe?

JAMIE: Scoop, that's the security guard. Look for famous people. Famous people, Scoop!

SCOOP: Got it. Oh! Oh, OH! You'll never believe who it is!

JAMIE: Who?!

SCOOP: It's Kim Gomez, the famous pop star!

JAMIE: See if you can get an interview!

SCOOP: Okay! Kim! Kim! Miss Gomez? *Scoop runs off stage.* OUCH!

JAMIE: What happened?

SCOOP: She turned and whipped her hair in my eye! KIM GOMEZ'S HAIR WAS IN MY EYE!!! This is the greatest job EVER!

JAMIE: Stay focused, Scoop. Who else is there? Do you see any other celebrities?

SCOOP: Yes. *Stares blankly.*

JAMIE: Who?

SCOOP: Oh! A lot of the celebrities are all talking together. It looks like Kim Gomez is talking with the famous athlete, JJ Rogers, and the movie star, Harrison Solo. Everyone who's anyone is here! Wait … I see … NO way!

JAMIE: Who?! Scoop, you have to actually report the news. You can't just watch it happen. Tell us what's going on!

SCOOP: Oh. Right. It's Joshua Reyes!

JAMIE: *Super excited.* WHO?! THE JOSHUA REYES?! Wow. That is amazing! My favorite rapper/singer/actor. He really does it all! Where is he? Who is he talking with? There's no way you could get an interview… He's too famous.

SCOOP: Actually, it looks like he's talking with a little boy who ran up to him. He's not even on the red carpet! Oh no! And it looks like the other celebrities are pointing and laughing at the little boy he's talking to.

JAMIE: Oh no! What is Joshua Reyes going to do?

SCOOP: I don't know who that little boy thinks he is. Like Joshua Reyes would want to talk to HIM! No way!

JAMIE: What's going on? What do you see?

SCOOP: Joshua Reyes is actually talking to him. AND TAKING A SELFIE WITH HIM!

Producer holds up "Awww" sign.

SCOOP: All of the other celebrities are still pointing and laughing. This could be the end of his career, Jamie.

JAMIE: What? No way a few lesser celebrities are going to mess with Reyes' career. He is more famous than all of them combined! See if you can get an interview!

SCOOP: You think he'd talk to me? I'm just the coffee guy. Oh, I know! I'll find out what kind of coffee he wants, and then I'll see if I can bring him some tomorrow.

JAMIE: Forget the coffee already! You are our only field reporter right now. Now, go get that interview!

Joshua Reyes enters. Scoop stops him for an interview.

SCOOP: Excuse me, sir? Mr. Reyes?

REYES: Hi there. You can call me Joshua.

SCOOP: *To the Camera.* He said I can call him JOSHUA!

JAMIE: That's great! Now ask him some questions!

SCOOP: Mr. Reyes – I mean – Joshua, sir, sir Joshua, um… How do you like your coffee?

JAMIE: FORGET THE COFFEE!

REYES: It's no problem. I'll answer all your questions. I like my coffee no sugar, cinnamon-vanilla cream. How do you like yours?

SCOOP: I like my coffee black. No sugar, no cream. I do have one more question, though. Why did you talk with that little boy when you knew everyone else was laughing at him and at you?

REYES: I don't care much about what other people think about me. That little boy was very nice. He just wanted to take a selfie with me, so I took the time to take a picture with him. Besides, those other people haven't even tried to talk to me, yet. The way I see it, everyone is the same and deserves to be treated with love and care. I'm going to do what is right, to show love and care to everyone, no matter what anyone else thinks.

He exits.

SCOOP: Wow! You heard it here, first on JUMP NEWS! Joshua Reyes doesn't care! This is Scoop Blakely, reporting live!

JAMIE: That's not what he said! He said he will do what is right, no matter what. He said that everyone deserves to be treated with love and care. It doesn't matter how famous they are.

SCOOP: Right. That's what I said!

JAMIE: Thank you for joining us here at JUMP NEWS. This is Jamie Jamison, signing off. Remember, when life hands you lemons, check for mold.

SFX: NEWS TRANSITION MUSIC

Video: Commercial

SONG *Lead the congregation in a fun worship song.*

MEMORY VERSE VIDEO

MEMORY VERSE

Our memory verse is from the book of Luke, chapter four, verses eighteen and nineteen. In these verses, Jesus is reading from the book of Isaiah. These verses are about Jesus!

Read the verses with me. **Luke 4:18-19 "The Spirit of the LORD is upon me, for he has anointed me to bring Good News to the poor. He has sent me to proclaim that captives will be released, that the blind will see, that the oppressed will be set free, and that the time of the LORD's favor has come."**

The Good News is that Jesus made a way for us to have a right relationship with God. Jesus is the best news the world has ever received! Let's review the motions to the first part of this verse.

Repeat after me.
Luke 4:18-19 *(Luke 4:18-19)*
"The Spirit of the LORD *(The Spirit of the LORD)*
is upon me *(is upon me)*,
for he has anointed me *(for he has anointed me)*
to bring Good News *(to bring Good News)*
to the poor *(to the poor)*."

Great job! Let's make motions for the next part of this verse. *(Make motions for the key words and phrases in the next part of the verse. Use these motions each time you say the verse.)*

Repeat after me.
"He has sent me *(He has sent me)*
to proclaim *(to proclaim)*
that captives *(that captives)*
will be released *(will be released)* … "

Now let's say everything we have learned together, starting with "Luke 4:18-19" on the count of three. One, two, three: **Luke 4:18-19 "The Spirit of the LORD is upon me, for he has anointed me to bring Good News to the poor. He has sent me to proclaim that captives will be released … "**

Great job! Even though our sin makes us like captives, Jesus came to set us free from the punishment for our wrong choices. Jesus is the best news the world has ever received! I challenge you to tell someone the Good News about Jesus this week.

ANNOUNCEMENTS

Use this time to encourage kids to bring friends and participate in whatever you may have coming up next.

REVIEW GAME

It's time for the REVIEW GAME!! I need one volunteer from each grade to come up on stage. I will choose people who have been listening and paying attention the whole service and want to play in our game.

Choose contestants and introduce them to the group in game show style.

During this game, your grade can win by getting very quiet when you hear the wrong answer and very loud when you hear the right answer. Each grade is going to have a different silly move and sound that you must do when you think you hear the right answer. (*Let your contestants choose a silly motion and sound for their grade.*)

I hope you are ready. I hope you have been paying attention, because the game begins ... NOW!

Give kids the opportunity to do their motions and silly sounds when they hear the correct answer. Award points to the grade who is the quietest when they hear the wrong answer and participates the most when they hear the right answer.

Question 1: What was today's Main Point?
a. Wow! That's Some Interesting News.
b. I Should Love Some People More than Others.
c. Jesus Loves Me, So I Can Love Others.
d. When Life Hands You Lemons, Check for Mold.

Question 2: Where can you find today's Bible lesson?
a. Matthew 7:36-50
b. Mark 7:36-50
c. Luke 7:36-50
d. John 7:36-50

Question 3: Who was the only person to welcome Jesus to Simon's house?

a. Simon

c. The Woman

b. The Pharisees

d. Simon's Servant

Question 4: Will Jesus' love ever run out?

a. Yes

c. Maybe

b. No

d. What? I wasn't paying attention.

Question 5: What did the woman use to wash Jesus' feet?

a. Her hair and cheap perfume

c. A towel and cheap perfume

b. Her sweater and expensive perfume

d. Her hair and expensive perfume

Question 6: Luke 4:18b says, "He has sent me to proclaim that _____ will be _____ ..."

a. captives, released

c. captives, put in jail

b. free people, put in jail

d. tacos, served on Tuesdays

SONG

Lead the congregation in a fun worship song.

DISMISSAL

LESSON 3

BIBLE LESSON

THE GOOD SAMARITAN
Luke 10:25-37

MAIN POINT

LOVE YOUR NEIGHBOR.

MEMORY VERSE

LUKE 4:18-19 "The Spirit of the Lord is upon me, for he has anointed me to bring Good News to the poor. He has sent me to proclaim that captives will be released, that the blind will see, that the oppressed will be set free, and that the time of the Lord's favor has come."

LESSON 3
HIGHLIGHTS

SPIRITUAL CONNECTION

Jamie and Scoop report on a high school track competition that closely mirrors the Parable of the Good Samaritan in Luke 10. Surprisingly, Musain Molt's rival, Besse Bowen, stops to help him cross the finish line. We should always stop to love others, because everyone is our neighbor.

CHARACTERS

JAMIE JAMISON – former intern who becomes a serious reporter
SCOOP BLAKELY – former intern in charge of coffee who becomes a goofy news reporter
PRODUCER – in charge of running the show, commercial breaks, etc.
MUSAIN MOLT - runner   **BESSE BOWENS** - runner
TEAMMATE – runner   **MEDIC** – nurse or doctor at the marathon

COSTUMES

JAMIE JAMISON – Slacks, Button-down shirt, Tie
SCOOP BLAKELY – Slacks, Button-down shirt, Tie
PRODUCER – All black clothing with headset and clipboard
MUSAIN MOLT – Running gear   **BESSE BOWENS** – Running gear
TEAMMATE – Running gear   **MEDIC** – Scrubs, Nurse or doctor costume

SET

JUMP News Room – News desk, Two chairs, Camera
Marathon – Clear the area around your seats to be the "track." Set up a finish line on stage.

PROPS

Skit - Cue cards, Clipboard, Coffee cups, Papers/pencils for desk, Microphone, Finish line, Medical supplies
Lesson - 4 Styrofoam cups clearly labeled Priest, Levite, Samaritan, and Injured Man or Jew, Slush powder (also called water gel) put in the Priest and Levite cups, Snow powder put in the Samaritan cup, Water, Table, Paper towels

JUMP NEWS

LEADER DEVOTION

The lawyer's answer to his own question in verse 27 sums up the Ten Commandments perfectly. The first four commandments focus on loving God, and the last six focus on loving others. The lawyer must have known this and felt embarrassed to ask a question with such an obvious answer, so he asked Jesus for clarification. After all, the Jews had enemies and surely would not be asked to love their enemies by the Messiah, the promised King of the Jews. Had Jesus answered the way the lawyer anticipated, He surely would have been accused of preaching anarchy against Rome. But Jesus rarely answered as predicted.

Instead, Jesus told a story that blew away many Jewish stereotypes. Priests were held in high esteem by the Jews. They were set apart from the community to perform acts of worship in the temple as outlined in the Books of Law (Genesis - Deuteronomy). Over time, priests were also seen as prominent political leaders in the community. Known for their piety, it was difficult to imagine a priest ignoring someone in need of help. Levites were also known for their piety and involvement in the temple. Yet when faced with a messy problem, both the priest and the Levite passed by on the opposite side of the road. After all, no one was watching to witness their act of kindness, so why bother?

Samaritans, however, were largely hated by the Jews. Jews would often travel the long way around Samaria just to avoid going through *their* country. The Samaritan people came from those left behind after the Jewish exile to Babylon. The Jews left behind intermarried with neighboring ethnic groups and began to worship the idols of those groups, designating new places of worship. Therefore, the Jews thought of Samaritans as inferior. In addition, the Samaritans were the people responsible for the attacks on Nehemiah, as he rebuilt the walls of Jerusalem, when the Jews returned home from exile. But when asked whom God expects us to love, Jesus starred a loving Samaritan as His shining example of godly love.

Prejudice has no place in the Kingdom of God. God created us all and loves us all. Like the Samaritans, we have all sinned and all need a Savior who loves us enough to take the punishment we deserve. Perhaps you have trouble loving some of the more "trying" people around you. Commit to pray each day for those hard-to-love people. Ask God to teach you each day how to truly love Him and love others the way He intended.

PRE-SERVICE

Play fun music and videos as kids come into JUMP Worship. Skit characters Jamie and Scoop hold up various cue cards ("Applause," "Laugh," "Oooh," "Ahhh," "Oh no," etc.) during the music and videos, encouraging kids to participate.

COUNTDOWN VIDEO

JUMP Worship is starting! Lead the congregation in counting down. Worshiping together is fun, and we are ready to begin!

SONG

Lead the congregation in a fun worship song.

MAIN POINT VIDEO

WELCOME

Welcome to JUMP, where we worship God together! Does anyone remember what book of the Bible we are studying during our series, JUMP News? *(Luke)* Yes! Great job! We are studying Luke's collection of eye-witness accounts of Jesus' time on earth. We hear a lot of news stories every day, but in JUMP News we are learning about the greatest news of all time. Jesus is the best news the world has ever received! We should all tell the world about Jesus.

Our Main Point is "Love Your Neighbor." According to Jesus, everyone is our neighbor! We should love others like Jesus loves us. Let's make motions to help us remember our Main Point. *(Make motions for the Main Point. Have kids repeat the motions and Main Point with you.)*

Now turn to your neighbor and say, "Helloooo!" (*Helloooo!*)
Turn to your other neighbor and say, "How are ya?" (*How are ya?*)
Tell them your name. Introduce yourself. (*Kids introduce themselves.*)
Now say "Listen up!" (*Listen up!*)
"Love Your Neighbor." (*Love Your Neighbor.*)
Point to them and say, "You're my neighbor!" (*You're my neighbor!*)
Point to someone else and say, "You're my neighbor!" (*You're my neighbor!*)
Face me and say, "Love Your Neighbor." (*Love Your Neighbor.*)

Great job! I can't wait to open the Bible and learn more about loving our neighbors as we worship today. We have a few rules to help us worship God, to keep our focus on Him and Him alone. Rule number one is STAY QUIET. When someone is up here talking, we should all be listening. Some people can talk and hear at the same time. Hearing me is not why we are here in JUMP. God has something to say to you, and we want to listen to Him. We want to pay attention with our heads and our hearts as we worship God today. Show me what that should look and sound like. (*Wait for kids to be quiet.*) Great job! Listening will help us stay focused on God.

Our second rule is KEEP YOUR HANDS AND FEET TO YOURSELF. Focusing on God is very difficult when the people around you are messing with you. Don't distract the people around you from worshiping God! Keep your hands and feet to yourself.

Rule number three is STAND UP DURING SONGS. JUMP is not a show. We are here to worship God together, so be a part of what we are doing. Think about the words of the songs when you sing. Use your hands and feet to worship God, not to mess with your friends.

And finally, our fourth rule is — say it with me — HAVE FUN! We are going to have so much fun today! Now let's worship God by talking to Him in prayer. Bow your heads and close your eyes. Focus on God only as we talk to Him.

PRAY

Lead the congregation in prayer.

JUMP SKIT PART 1

See skit script beginning on page 50.

LESSON 3 SKIT
PART 1

THE GOOD SAMARITAN

LOVE YOUR NEIGHBOR.

Skit Intro Video

Welcome to JUMP NEWS with your news team: Weather with Wendy Storm, Traffic with Iona Ford, Sports with Will Wynn, Politics with Cam Pain, and news anchors, Justin Report and Johnny Onthespot.

SFX: NEWS TRANSITION MUSIC

JAMIE: Well, hello there! I'm Jamie Jamison, your JUMP NEWS reporter. Here to bring you the latest-breaking news that will pull at your heart strings and make your mind go, "Wow! That's some interesting news."

Producer holds up "Applause" sign.

JAMIE: We have so many things happening in the news today, it's truly hard to pick which ones to tell you about … So, I'll just tell you all of them! **Slide: Image of deer on screen.** Up first, we have reports that a runaway deer has blocked traffic completely on 8th Street. Oh dear, this could be a hoof problem! See what I did there? Dear, as in the "deer" in the road? Hoof as in a "huge" problem … I am hilarious!

Producer holds up "Laugh" sign.

Scoop runs on with multiple coffees.

SCOOP: I'm here! No worries! Scoop is here with a scoop of morning joe! Sorry I'm a little late. There was this deer blocking traffic on 8th Street, and I couldn't get around him and …

JAMIE: *Stays in news-anchor voice.* Scoop, I already reported that story.

SCOOP: What story? Oh, you mean you already told all the news anchors I might be late because of the deer? Well thank you very much! I was worried that those anchors might be a teensy bit upset I was running late, but you definitely got me out of that jam. Thanks Jam-E! See what I did there?! Now, let's start giving out these coffees! Intern Scoop saves the day with a cup of joe! Iona Ford … are you here, Iona? I have your coffee!!

JAMIE: *Stays in news anchor voice.* Scoop, don't you remember?

SCOOP: Oh yes, I'm not supposed to yell out their names! I'm supposed to hand-deliver their coffee to them. Goodness, that's like rule #2 in the Intern Handbook. How could I forget?

JAMIE: *Stays in news anchor voice.* No, I meant that you need to remember all the people you got coffee for are on vacation. All the news anchors and reporters are out, and you and I are the replacement news anchors. Jamie Jamison here!

SCOOP: *Freezes and stares at the camera.* I'm Scoop.

JAMIE: Now, I have exciting news for all you viewers out there – or as I like to call you, our JUMP NEWS family.

SCOOP: We have exciting news?

JAMIE: Absolutely, Scoop! We have some great news! Now, why don't you read those notes right in front of you and tell the viewers what it is?

SCOOP: Oh dear, oh dear, oh dear …

JAMIE: Nope, already reported the deer story, Scoop.

Producer holds up "Laugh" sign.

JAMIE: Ha-ha! I am on a roll! Why don't you check the next page?

SCOOP: *Scoop can't find the page, tosses papers everywhere.* I don't know what exciting news you're talking about!

JAMIE: No worries Scoop, what are friends for, if they're not there to report the story that you're supposed to report?

SCOOP: Well friends make you laugh, and listen to you when you cry, and go to the zoo with you and -

JAMIE: Scoop, it was just an analogy.

SCOOP: Right.

JAMIE: *Jamie continues to tell the story, in his news anchor voice, while Scoop gets captivated in the story and forgets the camera is on.* Now, here's today's breaking news. SFX: BREAKING NEWS Today is the marathon of all marathons.

Slide: Marathon image on screen.

SCOOP: A TV MARATHON?

JAMIE: Nope. It's an actual marathon.

SCOOP: What's an actual marathon?

JAMIE: I'm glad you asked, Scoop! A marathon is when you run 26.2 miles in a row, and you're competing against other runners to finish it fastest.

Producer holds up "Oooh" sign.

SCOOP: Why in the world would someone want to do that? Is there a bear chasing them?

JAMIE: I know it's hard to understand us athletes, Scoop – but it's just in our blood to compete and run! Now, the exciting news is that right here – in our town – is the National High School Marathon! This means the fastest runners from all the high schools in the nation will come here and compete in the marathon!

SCOOP: How many kids will be competing from each school?

JAMIE: I'm glad you asked, Scoop! Each school can send three runners to compete. The winner will be based on the total time of all three runners. So, the goal is to send your top students to compete, since their scores will be combined.

SCOOP: So, these kids will really have to work together and encourage each other, as they run. Am I getting that correct?

JAMIE: Absolutely, Scoop! And guess what? You are going to go live to the race and report to our viewers everything that happens!

SCOOP: Viewers?

JAMIE: Scoop, remember, we are live on television right now.

SCOOP: *Stares at the audience, terrified.* I forgot ...

JAMIE: We'll be back after this special report! And remember, you heard it here first with Jamie Jamison. When life gives you lemons, check for mold.

> **SFX: NEWS TRANSITION MUSIC**

Jamie and Scoop exit in opposite directions.

> **SONG** *Lead the congregation in a fun worship song.*

SPECIAL REPORT
FROM THE BIBLE

JUMP NEWS

BIBLE LESSON INTRO VIDEO

 ### INTRO

Welcome back to JUMP. Today our main point is "Love Your Neighbor." That sounds easy enough, right? We love a lot of things. I LOVE Italian food. I LOVE playing outside. I LOVE watching funny movies. When Jesus tells us to love others, He is talking about a different kind of love called "agape" love. "Agape"(ä-gä-pā) is the Greek word used to describe God's unconditional love. When we show someone "agape" love, we are showing them the love of God.

Unconditional love, God's love, is not always easy to give away to everyone. Sometimes, we meet people we just don't like. Sometimes, we meet people who are different from us. Sometimes, we meet people who are very, very mean to us. Does God really want us to show His love to EVERYONE?

 ### READ THE BIBLE

In **Luke 10: 25-29**, a lawyer asked Jesus that same question. The Law in the Bible says to "love your neighbor as yourself." Surely that didn't mean everyone, right? The lawyer asked Jesus to explain what the Law meant by "neighbor." Whom did he really HAVE to love?

To answer, Jesus told a parable. A parable is a made-up story that helps us understand important truths. Jesus' story started with a Jewish man on the road from Jericho. On the way, the man was attacked by robbers. The robbers beat him and left. They thought the man was dead. The man needed help.

Soon a priest came to the place where the man was lying. If someone were hurt on the side of the road, would you expect a pastor to help him? Of course! Pastors are supposed to show God's love to everyone. Surely the priest in Jesus' story would stop to help the man. But the priest passed by on the opposite side of the road.

Then a Levite came down the road. Levites were people who worked in the synagogues. Imagine someone who worked at a church saw a person hurt on the side of the road. Of course you would think the church worker would stop to help, but Jesus said that the Levite also walked by on the opposite side of the road.

Finally, a Samaritan walked down the road. Jews did not like Samaritans at all. In fact, the Jews hated the Samaritans so much, they would not even walk through Samaria on long trips. They would go the long way around just to avoid running into a Samaritan. Surely a Samaritan wouldn't help a Jewish man. But in Jesus' story, that is exactly what happened.

The Samaritan stopped to help the wounded man. He bandaged his wounds and put him on his donkey. Then the Samaritan took him to an inn and paid for his medical bills. Who in this story showed the injured man agape love, God's love?

The Samaritan showed God's love to a Jewish man, even though they were not friends.

 # OBJECT LESSON

God's love is for everyone, no exceptions. Imagine this water is God's love. God pours His love out on everyone the same. *Pour the water into the cup labeled "Priest."* God loves us so much and wants us to share His love with everyone. Unfortunately, the priest did not share God's love. *Turn the "Priest" cup upside down to try to pour it into the "Jew" cup. No water should come out.* Maybe the priest thought he was too busy to stop to help the man in need. For whatever reason, he did not share God's love.

Pour the water into the cup labeled "Levite." The Levite did not share God's love, either. Turn the "Levite" cup upside down to try to pour it into the "Jew" cup. No water should come out. The Priest and the Levite both talked about God's love. They both knew a lot about God. They were both people who did right when other people were looking. But when no one was looking, when it was just between them, the injured man, and God, they decided to keep walking. We don't know why they chose not to help the man. Were they too busy? Were they afraid of getting dirty? Were they hoping someone else would help him instead?

Unfortunately, we can be a lot like the priest and the Levite in this story. We sometimes make up all kinds of excuses not to show God's love to others.

"I don't need to share my pencils. They should have brought their own pencils to class."

"I don't want to play with him. He's so annoying! Nobody likes him, so why should I have to play with him at recess?"

"I don't want to help her. She's mean. She does not deserve it."

"I don't even know that guy. Why should I have to be nice to him?"

Jesus calls us to love our neighbors, and that means everyone - even the people we don't like. Instead of only showing God's love to people we like or feel comfortable around, Jesus wants us to be like the Good Samaritan. He poured out God's love to a stranger who did not like him at all. *Pour the water into the "Samaritan" cup, then pour out the snow into the "Injured Man" or "Jew" cup.*

 ## APPLICATION

This week, ask God to teach you to love others the way He loves them. Ask Him to show you how you can be a part of spreading the best news the world has ever received. Let's take the challenge to share God's love with everyone we see - with our family members, with our friends, with bullies, even with people at the grocery store!

PRAY

OFFERING SONG

Lead the congregation in a slower worship song.

JUMP SKIT PART 2

See skit script beginning on page 56.

LOVE YOUR NEIGHBOR.

JUMP NEWS

LESSON 3 SKIT
PART 2

THE GOOD SAMARITAN

LOVE YOUR NEIGHBOR.

Skit Intro Video

Welcome to JUMP NEWS with your news team: Weather with Wendy Storm, Traffic with Iona Ford, Sports with Will Wynn, Politics with Cam Pain, and news anchors, Justin Report and Johnny Onthespot.

SFX: NEWS TRANSITION MUSIC

JAMIE: Welcome back to JUMP NEWS, I'm Jamie Jamison.

Producer holds up "Applause" sign.

JAMIE: We have Scoop Blakely live in the field with this fascinating story. What's the scoop, Scoop?

Lights up on Scoop standing next to a "Finish Line" banner. Scoop is interrupted by runners during the broadcast.

SCOOP: This is Scoop Blakely reporting live from National High School Marathon, where the fastest runners from all over the USA are here to compete with their fellow classmates for the fastest team time. Now, there are a couple of schools to keep our eyes on. You see, Antelope High School has Musain Molt on their team. He is potentially the fastest high school runner ever. However, Musain has some competition with up and coming Besse Bowens from Cheetah Charter School. Critics believe that both Besse and Musain are going to be leading their teams to victory today with their fast speeds, but we'll just have to wait and see what happens.

JAMIE: Scoop, I want you to keep your eyes on these two runners. They are surely going to be breaking records today, and we want to catch it all live here at JUMP NEWS!

SCOOP: Got it. **SFX: STARTING GUN**

JAMIE: Sounds like the race has begun!

SCOOP: That's right, Jamie! *Looks off backstage.* The marathon is underway! Wow, it looks like they just passed mile 1!

JAMIE: That was incredibly fast!

SCOOP: Well, these are the fastest racers in the US of A!

JAMIE: You're absolutely right, Scoop!

SCOOP: Oh, this is too exciting - Musain Molt is at mile 25 and approaching the finish line!

JAMIE: The runners are already at mile 25?

SCOOP: They're fast I tell you, very fast.

Musain runs on stage and immediately trips just before the finish line.

SCOOP: This is breaking news!

JAMIE: What is it, Scoop? Tell us! Tell us!

SCOOP: It appears that Musain Molt has fallen down and is in incredible pain!

SFX: DUN DUN DUN

Producer holds up "Oh No!" Sign.

JAMIE: My my my. This is not good. But it is good for our ratings, as people are tuning in right now to our live broadcast of Musain Molt who just fell in the National High School Marathon.

SCOOP: Oh look! The medic is on the way! I'm sure he'll stop to help him! What are medics for besides helping fallen athletes?

Medic runs on and keeps going.

SCOOP: I can't believe my eyes. The medic was so distracted with the race, that he didn't stop to look down and see Musain in pain. What a shame. Oh look, one of Musain's teammates is coming – I'm sure he'll stop to help Musain, so they can cross the finish line together!

Teammate runs by and doesn't stop.

SCOOP: I am just shocked. Mussain's teammate didn't stop to help!!! All he cared about was his own time and didn't care to help his wounded friend. This is unbelievable, Jamie.

JAMIE: This truly is BREAKING NEWS. Ha-ha! Do you get it? Because his leg is broken …

SCOOP: Oh, now Besse Bowens is about to run by. I know she won't stop to help, considering Musain is her main competition today. I'm sure she wants nothing more than to beat Musain Molt in this race and bring her Cheetah Charter School to #1 high school in the USA!

JAMIE: I believe you are right, Scoop. There is NO way she'll stop to help.

Besse runs on and stops to help Musain stand.

SCOOP: Wait.

JAMIE: What's going on? What do you see?

SCOOP: Besse has stopped to help Musain up! Now she's helping him finish the race!!! Wow!! That was the exact opposite of what I thought would happen!

JAMIE: This is incredible BREAKING NEWS!

SCOOP: I truly thought she'd be the last person to help Musain.

JAMIE: You know, Scoop, this reminds me of the special report we heard today about the Good Samaritan. Besse is a lot like the man who showed mercy on the one who was attacked by robbers. She showed mercy on Musain just like the man in our story. We are all called to be like Besse and love our neighbor!!

SCOOP: This marathon has been epic – one that will go down in National High School Marathon history.

JAMIE: That's right, SCOOP. Thanks for your excellent reporting and thank you viewers for joining us here at JUMP NEWS. This is Jamie Jamison, signing off. Remember, when life hands you lemons, check for mold.

SFX: NEWS TRANSITION MUSIC

Video: Commercial

SONG *Lead the congregation in a fun worship song.*

MEMORY VERSE VIDEO

MEMORY VERSE

Our memory verse is from the book of Luke, chapter four, verses eighteen and nineteen. These verses are about Jesus!

Read the verses with me. **Luke 4:18-19 "The Spirit of the LORD is upon me, for he has anointed me to bring Good News to the poor. He has sent me to proclaim that captives will be released, that the blind will see, that the oppressed will be set free, and that the time of the LORD's favor has come."**

The Good News is that Jesus made a way for us to have a right relationship with God. Jesus is the best news the world has ever received! Let's review the motions to the first part of this verse.

Repeat after me.
Luke 4:18-19 *(Luke 4:18-19)*
"The Spirit of the LORD is upon me *(The Spirit of the LORD is upon me)*,
for he has anointed me to bring *(for he has anointed me to bring)*
Good News to the poor *(Good News to the poor)*.
He has sent me to proclaim *(He has sent me to proclaim)*
that captives will be released *(that captives will be released)* ... "

Great job! Let's make motions for the next part of this verse. *(Make motions for the key words and phrases in the next part of the verse. Use these motions each time you say the verse.)*

Repeat after me:
" ... that the blind *(that the blind)*
will see *(will see)* ... "

Now stand up and let's say everything we have learned together, starting with "Luke 4:18-19" on the count of three. One, two, three: **Luke 4:18-19 "The Spirit of the LORD is upon me, for he has anointed me to bring Good News to the poor. He has sent me to proclaim that captives will be released, that the blind will see ... "**

Great job! Jesus healed people who were physically blind. He also heals people who have been blind to their big sin problem. Jesus is the best news the world has ever received, and this news is for everybody! I challenge you to tell someone the Good News about Jesus this week.

ANNOUNCEMENTS

Use this time to encourage kids to bring friends and participate in whatever you may have coming up next.

REVIEW GAME

It's time for the REVIEW GAME!! I need one volunteer from each grade to come up on stage. I will choose people who have been listening and paying attention the whole service and want to play in our game.

Choose contestants and introduce them to the group in game show style.

During this game, your grade can win by getting very quiet when you hear the wrong answer and very loud when you hear the right answer. Each grade is going to have a different silly move and sound that you must do when you think you hear the right answer. (*Let your contestants choose a silly motion and sound for their grade.*)

I hope you are ready. I hope you have been paying attention, because the game begins ... NOW!

Give kids the opportunity to do their motions and silly sounds when they hear the correct answer. Award points to the grade who is the quietest when they hear the wrong answer and participates the most when they hear the right answer.

Question 1: What was today's Main Point?
a. Love Your Pizza.
b. Love Your Family.
c. Love Your Neighbor.
d. When Life Hands You Lemons, Check for Mold.

Question 2: Where can you find today's Bible lesson?
a. Samaria 10:25-37
b. Leotta 10:25-37
c. Luke 10:25-37
d. Luke 4:18-19

Question 3: What did the priest do when he saw the injured man?

    a. Helped him

    b. Prayed for him

    c. Crossed to the other side of the road

    d. Told a chicken joke

For added fun, play "The Chicken Dance" each time you read a wrong answer about chickens. Act bewildered, like you do not know where the music is coming from. Read the question again and continue.

Question 4: What did the Levite (Temple assistant) do when he saw the injured man?

    a. Helped him

    b. Referred him to a doctor

    c. Crossed to the other side of the road

    d. Did the chicken dance

Question 5: What did the Samaritan do when he saw the injured man?

    a. Helped him

    b. Called him mean names

    c. Crossed to the other side of the road

    d. Ran away to buy a chicken

Question 6: Luke 4:18b says, "...He has sent me to proclaim that captives will be released, that the _____ will _____ ..."

    a. blind, see

    b. free people, be put in jail

    c. seeing, go blind

    d. tacos, be served on Tuesdays

SONG

Lead the congregation in a fun worship song.

DISMISSAL

JESUS IS THE

BEST

NEWS THE
WORLD HAS
EVER RECEIVED

LESSON 4

BIBLE LESSON

MARY AND MARTHA
Luke 10:38-42

MAIN POINT

JESUS WANTS TO SPEND TIME WITH US.

MEMORY VERSE

LUKE 4:18-19 "The Spirit of the Lord is upon me, for he has anointed me to bring Good News to the poor. He has sent me to proclaim that captives will be released, that the blind will see, that the oppressed will be set free, and that the time of the Lord's favor has come."

LESSON 4
HIGHLIGHTS

SPIRITUAL CONNECTION

Jamie and Scoop report on an exclusive Taylor Fast party, but Scoop gets distracted by the party food. Like Martha missed an opportunity to spend time with Jesus, Scoop missed an opportunity to meet Taylor Fast.

CHARACTERS

JAMIE JAMISON – former intern who becomes a serious reporter

SCOOP BLAKELY – former intern in charge of coffee who becomes a goofy news reporter

PRODUCER – in charge of running the show, commercial breaks, etc.

COSTUMES

JAMIE JAMISON – Slacks, Button-down shirt, Tie

SCOOP BLAKELY – Slacks, Button-down shirt, Tie

PRODUCER – All black clothing with headset and clipboard

SET

JUMP News Room – News desk, Two chairs, Camera

Taylor Fast Party – Red rope stanchions

PROPS

Skit - Cue cards, Clipboard, Coffee cups, Papers/pencils for desk, Microphone, Chocolate Cake, Popcorn

Lesson - Loud music and videos

LEADER DEVOTION

The story of Mary and Martha's visit with their friend, Jesus, is often wrongly used to compare and contrast a contemplative personality with a more hands-on, hard-working personality. Good works are the fruit of a right relationship with God, as we choose to love others the way Christ has loved us (Galatians 5:22-25; 1 John 2:6). We have been called to do our best, in everything we do, to the glory of God, regardless of personality (Colossians 3:17). We have not, however, been called to compare ourselves to others or to do this work under our own power as a means to gain favor with God.

Martha was so distracted by what she saw as her sister's inaction, she tattled to Jesus. She allowed her anger towards Mary to interfere with her focus on the Lord. How often do we waste our thoughts on the actions of others or comparing ourselves to others? The comparison game never ends well. Comparing ourselves to others almost always results in a wrong understanding of our relationship with the Lord. Your relationship with God has nothing to do with anyone else. Your relationship with God is between you and Him. He will not love you more, because you have served Him more than others. God loves you right now with all the love He has. There is nothing you, or anyone else, can do to make Him love you more, and there is nothing you, or anyone else, can do to make Him love you less.

Martha was working to serve Jesus, and Mary was endeavoring to know Him. Knowing Jesus must be the priority in every Christan's life. It is infinitely more important to live "in" Christ than to live "for" Him. His invitation to join Him in His work is not our cue to start working under our own power. Our good works should always be an outpouring of our relationship with Christ (John 15). Our relationship with Christ is the foundation of the Christian life.

Good works without the foundation of a growing relationship with Jesus is a sure recipe for burnout. Remember, an empty cup cannot pour into anyone. Take time this week to allow Jesus to pour into you, so you can in turn pour into others. Ask God to identify distractions in your life that take your focus off Him, so you can spend time with Jesus - not as a task on a "to do" list of good works, but as an opportunity to get to know the One who unconditionally loves you more than anyone else can.

PRE-SERVICE

Play fun music and videos as kids come into JUMP Worship. Skit characters Jamie and Scoop hold up various cue cards ("Applause," "Laugh," "Oooh," "Ahhh," "Oh no," etc.) during the music and videos, encouraging kids to participate.

COUNTDOWN VIDEO

JUMP Worship is starting! Lead the congregation in counting down. Worshiping together is fun, and we are ready to begin!

SONG

Lead the congregation in a fun worship song.

MAIN POINT VIDEO

WELCOME

Welcome to JUMP, where we worship God together! Does anyone remember what book of the Bible we are studying during our series, JUMP News? *(Luke)* Yes! Great job! We are studying Luke's collection of eye-witness accounts of Jesus' time on earth. We hear a lot of news stories every day, but in JUMP News we are learning about the greatest news of all time. Jesus is the best news the world has ever received! We should all tell the world about Jesus.

Our Main Point is "Jesus Wants to Spend Time with Us." We get to spend time with Jesus right now as we choose to worship Him. When we worship Jesus, we choose to put Him first, to focus our hearts and minds completely on Him. Isn't it great that Jesus, the Son of God, wants to spend time with us, too?!

Let's make motions to help us remember our Main Point. *(Make motions for the Main Point. Have kids repeat the motions and Main Point with you.)*

Now turn to your neighbor and say, "Hi!" *(Hi!)*
Turn to your other neighbor and say, "Wake up!" *(Wake up!)*
Tell them your name. Introduce yourself. *(Kids introduce themselves.)*
Now say "This is important!" *(This is important!)*
"Jesus Wants to Spend Time with Us." *(Jesus Wants to Spend Time with Us.)*
Point to them and say, "Jesus Wants to Spend Time with You!" *(Jesus Wants to Spend Time with You!)*
Point to someone else and say, "Jesus Wants to Spend Time with You Too!" *(Jesus Wants to Spend Time with You Too!)*
Face me and say, "Jesus Wants to Spend Time with Us." *(Jesus Wants to Spend Time with Us.)*

Great job! I can't wait to open the Bible and spend time with Jesus as we worship today. We have a few rules to help us worship the Lord, to keep our focus on Him and Him alone. Rule number one is STAY QUIET. When someone is up here talking, we should all be listening. Some people can talk and hear at the same time. Hearing me is not why we are here in JUMP. God has something to say to you, and we want to listen to Him. We want to pay attention with our heads and our hearts as we worship God today. Show me what that should look and sound like. *(Wait for kids to be quiet.)* Great job! Listening will help us stay focused on God.

Our second rule is KEEP YOUR HANDS AND FEET TO YOURSELF. Focusing on God is very difficult when the people around you are messing with you. Don't distract the people around you from worshiping God! Keep your hands and feet to yourself.

Rule number three is STAND UP DURING SONGS. JUMP is not a show. We are here to worship God together, so be a part of what we are doing. Think about the words of the songs when you sing. Use your hands and feet to worship God, not to mess with your friends.

And finally, our fourth rule is – say it with me – HAVE FUN! We are going to have so much fun today! Now let's worship God by talking to Him in prayer. Bow your heads and close your eyes. Focus on God only as we spend time with Him and talk to Him.

PRAY

Lead the congregation in prayer.

JUMP SKIT PART 1

See skit script beginning on page 68.

LESSON 4 SKIT
PART 1
MARY AND MARTHA

JESUS WANTS TO SPEND TIME WITH US.

Skit Intro Video

Welcome to JUMP NEWS with your news team: Weather with Wendy Storm, Traffic with Iona Ford, Sports with Will Wynn, Politics with Cam Pain, and news anchors, Justin Report and Johnny Onthespot.

SFX: NEWS TRANSITION MUSIC

JAMIE: Welcome back to your favorite news station – JUMP NEWS! I'm Jamie Jamison, your JUMP NEWS reporter. Here to bring you the latest-breaking news that will pull at your heart strings and make your mind go, "Wow! That's some interesting news."

Producer holds up "Applause" sign.

JAMIE: Scoop Blakely and I will bring you the latest breaking news to keep you up to date with the world around you.

Scoop runs on with multiple coffees.

SCOOP: It's coffee time everybody! I'm here. I'm on time. And I've got your coffee! Today is going wonderfully so far! The sun is shining, there's a cool breeze in the air, the birds are singing, and I'm doing my job as the news intern by getting all the news anchors their favorite coffee.

JAMIE: *Stays in news anchor voice.* Scoop, it is a wonderful day outside; you are absolutely right. Now, why don't you turn and say 'hello' to our viewers?

SCOOP: Viewers?

JAMIE: *Stays in news anchor voice.* Scoop, don't you remember?

SCOOP: No.

JAMIE: *Stays in news anchor voice.* Remember, Scoop? All the people you got coffee for are on vacation. All the news anchors and reporters are out, and you and I are the replacement news anchors. Jamie Jamison here!

SCOOP: *Freezes and stares at the camera.* I'm Scoop.

JAMIE: I've got exciting news for all you viewers out there – or as I like to call you, our JUMP NEWS family.

SCOOP: Oh, are you telling them about the oldest woman alive, who eats bacon every day? Now that sounds delicious!

JAMIE: Nope, that wasn't what I was going to report – but that is actually interesting news.

SCOOP: Oh, are you going to tell them about the little mouse that dragged an entire slice of pizza down some stairs?

JAMIE: Nope, not reporting on that either – but that is a cute story.

SCOOP: Oh, I know, I know! You're going to tell them about the man who broke the Guinness Book of World Records for the largest onion, weighing in at 17 lbs. and 15.5 ounces.

Producer holds up "Oh My!" sign.

JAMIE: No, Scoop. That's not the story. But seriously, I'm impressed. Where have you been learning all these stories?

SCOOP: Oh, I've just been reading the newspaper.

JAMIE: I didn't know people still did that.

SCOOP: Well, I like to stay up-to-date with current events, Jamie.

JAMIE: Who are you, and what did you do with Scoop? *Jamie does a fake laugh.* Now, let me tell you the breaking news. <mark>SFX: BREAKING NEWS STORY</mark> The wealthiest people in the whole world are joining together for the finest dinner party to ever exist.

SCOOP: No way! Do I know any of these wealthy people?

JAMIE: I don't think so, Scoop. These people are wealthy, but they aren't exactly well known. They are owners of different oil companies and car corporations.

SCOOP: Then why, exactly, are we reporting on this story?

JAMIE: I'm glad you asked! We are reporting this story, because one incredibly popular celebrity will be in attendance. THE Taylor Fast.

SCOOP: Wait. THE TAYLOR FAST? You mean the singer, celebrity, most Instagram followers, kind to everyone she meets, Taylor Fast?

JAMIE: That's right! I knew you'd be excited! And here's more exciting news for you and our viewers at home. This dinner party has said they will allow only ONE news reporter inside the home and, guess what?

SCOOP: You're going?

JAMIE: No, Scoop! You, as our fill-in news reporter, are the only one who gets to go inside to report to the world what happens at this party and more importantly, to catch an interview with THE TAYLOR FAST!

SCOOP: *Over excited.* There's no way! I get to meet Taylor Fast?! I get to go to the finest dinner party in all the land and meet THE TAYLOR FAST? Is it too much to wear a t-shirt with her picture on it? Or just a knitted sweater? I have to get her autograph. Maybe I'll bring a CD of me singing, and she can listen to it, and I can join her band!

JAMIE: Calm down, Scoop. You're still on TV, and you are a reporter. You're going to go in there and get that interview with Taylor Fast, and then come back outside of the house, and report to all of us what she said.

SCOOP: YOU GOT IT! This is the best internship ever!

JAMIE: We'll be back after this special report!

SFX: NEWS TRANSITION MUSIC

Jamie and Scoop exit in different directions.

SONG *Lead the congregation in a fun worship song.*

SPECIAL REPORT
FROM THE BIBLE JUMP NEWS

BIBLE LESSON INTRO VIDEO

 INTRO

Hi, everybody! I'm so glad you're here today. I want to start off by telling you a story. Listen closely, because I'm going to ask questions in just a minute to see how well you listened.

One time ... *(Tell a relatively short personal story.)*

Have the tech team start playing funny videos, loud music, and crazy lights while you continue your story. Do not yell over the noise, but continue to speak in a regular tone throughout the story.

When your story is over, signal the tech team to stop the videos, music, and lights.

Ask a few questions about the story you told.

You don't know the answers to my questions? Why? Was something distracting you?

It's hard to listen when everything around you is going crazy. Today, we are learning that Jesus wants to spend time with us. In the middle of our crazy lives, Jesus wants us to take time to focus on Him, to simply hang out with Him.

 READ THE BIBLE

Luke 10:38-42 tells us about one of the times Jesus went to visit His good friends Mary, Martha, and their brother, Lazarus. Jesus went to His friends' house to spend time with them. Try to picture Jesus hanging out in your living room. That would be so amazing! Everyone was excited Jesus was there.

Read Luke 10:38-40.

Have you ever had to clean your house before company came? Cleaning for friends to come can be a lot of work. You have to clean the living room, the bedrooms, the bathrooms, the kitchen - everything. Then you have to make sure there is enough food for everyone. There is a lot of work to do before company comes to your house!

Usually, though, the work stops as soon as your friends arrive. Once they are in your house, you stop working and start spending time with your friends and family. Can you imagine inviting guests over and then vacuuming the whole time they are there? That would not make much sense.

When Mary saw Jesus, she stopped what she was doing to spend time with Him. Martha kept working. Then Martha started to get angry. Why should she have to do all the work by herself? So, Martha did what so many of us do when we are upset: she tattled on her sister. She wanted Jesus to tell her sister to get up and help her around the house, but that's not what Jesus did.

Read Luke 10:41-42.

Jesus came to spend time with His friends. He was not going to tell His friends to stop spending time with Him. Martha was so distracted with her work and with her frustration with Mary, she missed an opportunity to spend time with Jesus. Jesus gently reminded His friend, Martha, that spending time with Him was much better.

 # APPLICATION

Jesus wants to spend time with us, too. He wants us to get to know Him. Jesus wants to listen to us in prayer. He wants us to listen to Him in prayer, too. He wants to speak to us through the Bible and through other Christians. Unfortunately, we often become so distracted with everything else going on in our daily lives that we miss out on these opportunities to spend time with Jesus.

What is distracting you from spending time with Jesus? Are you so frustrated with someone that it's hard to focus on Him? Ask Jesus to help you. Are you too busy? Maybe you need to schedule time to be alone and quiet with Jesus.

Let's choose to stop and focus on Jesus, because Jesus, the King of kings, wants to spend time with us.

PRAY

OFFERING SONG

Lead the congregation in a slower worship song.

JUMP SKIT PART 2

See skit script beginning on page 74.

JESUS WANTS TO SPEND TIME WITH US.

JUMP NEWS

LESSON 4 SKIT
PART 2
MARY AND MARTHA

JESUS WANTS TO SPEND TIME WITH US.

Skit Intro Video

Welcome to JUMP NEWS with your news team: Weather with Wendy Storm, Traffic with Iona Ford, Sports with Will Wynn, Politics with Cam Pain, and news anchors, Justin Report and Johnny Onthespot.

SFX: NEWS TRANSITION MUSIC

JAMIE: Welcome back to JUMP NEWS, I'm Jamie Jamison.

Producer holds up "Applause" sign.

JAMIE: We have Scoop Blakely live in the field. What's the scoop, Scoop?

Lights up on Scoop standing next to rope stanchions.

SCOOP: This is Scoop Blakely, here to give you the scoop! I'm reporting live from outside the house of the finest dinner party in the world. Right now, inside this house, there are people from all over the world! These people have done great things – but none of them are as great as THE TAYLOR FAST!

JAMIE: That's right, Scoop! Now, we want you to go inside, and take your phone with you. Take photos of Taylor interacting with the guests. Take photos of what she's wearing and everything she does. We are the ONLY news station to report on this, so let's give our viewers what they want!

SCOOP: Got it. *Scoop runs offstage.*

Slide: 5 minutes later.

Scoop runs back onstage.

JAMIE: So, tell us what you saw!

SCOOP: OH JAMIE! You wouldn't believe it! THE Taylor Fast is inside, and guess what?! SO IS THE GREATEST JELL-O MOLD YOU HAVE EVER SEEN! I got a photo of it to show you all.

Slide: Image of Jell-O mold.

JAMIE: Scoop, that's great, but we want images of Taylor Fast. And we want you to get an interview with her. Can you do that?

SCOOP: Oh, right. Yes. Got it. *Scoop runs offstage.*

Slide: 5 minutes later.

Scoop runs back onstage with chocolate on face.

JAMIE: So tell us, and the viewers, what you saw!

SCOOP: Oh, this is too exciting! *Says while eating cake.* They have the best chocolate cake EVER!

Slide: mage of chocolate cake.

JAMIE: Scoop! We need to know about Taylor. Did she eat the cake too?

SCOOP: Oh, umm … Taylor, Taylor … Did she eat the cake? Umm … I mean, she probably did? It's amazing! Who wouldn't eat this cake?

JAMIE: Scoop, we need FACTS! Not just assumptions! Go in there and take a picture with Taylor Fast!!!

SCOOP: Got it. I won't get distracted this time! *Scoop runs offstage.*

Slide: 5 minutes later.

Scoop runs back onstage with popcorn and spills it everywhere.

JAMIE: So, tell us, the viewers and me, what you saw!

SCOOP: You wouldn't believe it!

JAMIE: What? Did Taylor do something super kind and generous?! That's so Taylor …

SCOOP: Oh, I don't know about Taylor. But they have the biggest assortment of popcorn you've ever seen! Buttered, caramel, cheese, chocolate covered …

JAMIE: Scoop, I need you to listen. You keep getting distracted from the most important thing. Remember, you're supposed to spend time with Taylor Fast. Ask her questions. Listen to her stories. But instead, you've stayed busy with all the other things going on – chocolate, Jell-O, popcorn. You know, this reminds me of the special report we heard earlier. You are acting like Martha, who got distracted with all the tasks of the dinner party and forgot to spend time with the most important person in the room – Jesus. But Mary knew to spend time with Jesus and to listen to His stories. Now, I need you to go back in there and spend time with Taylor. Can you do that?

SCOOP: Got it. I won't get distracted this time! I want to spend time with Taylor just like Mary spent time with Jesus. Let's do this! I'll be back after this commercial break with the latest breaking news on Taylor Fast!

JAMIE: Thanks for your excellent reporting, Scoop. And thank you, viewers, for joining us. This has been JUMP NEWS with Jamie Jamison and Scoop Blakely. Remember, when life hands you lemons, check for mold.

SFX: NEWS TRANSITION MUSIC

Video: Commercial

SONG *Lead the congregation in a fun worship song.*

MEMORY VERSE VIDEO

MEMORY VERSE

Our memory verse is from the book of Luke, chapter four, verses eighteen and nineteen. These verses are about Jesus!

Read the verses with me. **Luke 4:18-19 "The Spirit of the LORD is upon me, for he has anointed me to bring Good News to the poor. He has sent me to proclaim that captives will be released, that the blind will see, that the oppressed will be set free, and that the time of the LORD's favor has come."**

The Good News is that Jesus made a way for us to have a right relationship with God. Jesus is the best news the world has ever received! Let's review the motions to the first part of this verse.

Repeat after me.
Luke 4:18-19 *(Luke 4:18-19)*
"The Spirit of the LORD is upon me *(The Spirit of the LORD is upon me)*,
for he has anointed me to bring *(for he has anointed me to bring)*
Good News to the poor *(Good News to the poor)*.
He has sent me to proclaim *(He has sent me to proclaim)*
that captives will be released *(that captives will be released)*,
that the blind will see *(that the blind will see)* … "

Great job! In today's Bible story, Martha was too busy cleaning and worrying about her sister to focus on Jesus. Jesus wanted to spend time with her, but Martha let other things get in the way. Let's not let anything distract us from spending time with Jesus by memorizing God's Word. Just for fun, let's see if we can say the verse together without getting distracted by the sounds and lights in the room.

SFX: FUNNY MUSIC

Flash lights off and on in a semi-random pattern as kids recite the verse together.

That was really difficult! Now let's see if we can say the verse without looking at the screens.

Take the verse off the screens.

Stand up and let's say everything we have learned together, starting with "Luke 4:18-19" on the count of three. One, two, three: **Luke 4:18-19 "The Spirit of the LORD is upon me, for he has anointed me to bring Good News to the poor. He has sent me to proclaim that captives will be released, that the blind will see … "**

Great job! Jesus is the best news the world has ever received! I challenge you to tell someone the Good News about Jesus this week.

ANNOUNCEMENTS

Use this time to encourage kids to bring friends and participate in whatever you may have coming up next.

REVIEW GAME

It's time for the REVIEW GAME!! I need one volunteer from each grade to come up on stage. I will choose people who have been listening and paying attention the whole service and want to play in our game.

Choose contestants and introduce them to the group in game show style.

During this game, your grade can win by getting very quiet when you hear the wrong answer and very loud when you hear the right answer. Each grade is going to have a different silly move and sound that you must do when you think you hear the right answer. (*Let your contestants choose a silly motion and sound for their grade.*)

I hope you are ready. I hope you have been paying attention, because the game begins … NOW!

Give kids the opportunity to do their motions and silly sounds when they hear the correct answer. Award points to the grade who is the quietest when they hear the wrong answer and participates the most when they hear the right answer.

Question 1: What was today's Main Point?
a. Grandma Wants to Spend Time with Us.
b. Jesus Wants to Spend Time with Us.
c. Doing Work Is Bad.
d. When Life Hands You Lemons, Check for Mold.

Question 2: Where can you find today's Bible lesson?
a. Martha 10:38-42 **c. Luke 10:38-42**
b. Mark 10:38-42 d. Luke 2

Question 3: What did Mary do when Jesus came to visit?
a. Swept the floors **c. Spent time with Jesus**
b. Performed a talent show d. Told a chicken joke

For added fun, play "The Chicken Dance" each time you read a wrong answer about chickens. Act bewildered, like you do not know where the music is coming from. Read the question again and continue.

Question 4: What did Martha do when Jesus came to visit?
a. Cooking and cleaning c. Fainted
b. Spent time with Jesus d. Did the chicken dance

Question 5: When Martha complained, what did Jesus say?
a. Mary was going to get in trouble. c. Martha was going to get in trouble.
b. Mary chose what was better. d. Martha should buy a chicken.

Question 6: Luke 4:18b says, "He has sent me to proclaim that captives will be released, that the _____ will _____ …"
a. blind, see c. seeing, go blind
b. free people, be put in jail d. tacos, be served on Tuesdays

SONG

Lead the congregation in a fun worship song.

DISMISSAL

REPORTING
LIVE
FROM THE
BOOK OF LUKE

LESSON 5

BIBLE LESSON

THE PRODIGAL SON
Luke 15:11-32

MAIN POINT

JESUS FORGIVES SINNERS LIKE ME.

MEMORY VERSE

LUKE 4:18-19 "The Spirit of the Lord is upon me, for he has anointed me to bring Good News to the poor. He has sent me to proclaim that captives will be released, that the blind will see, that the oppressed will be set free, and that the time of the Lord's favor has come."

JUMP NEWS

HIGHLIGHTS

SPIRITUAL CONNECTION

Jamie and Scoop report on a big soccer match in Italy. When Scoop wastes his ticket money on food, he is unable to go to the game. Although he deserves to be fired, Jamie gladly accepts him back into the newsroom. Like the prodigal son, we have sinned. Although we do not deserve Heaven, Jesus forgives us. He made a way for us to be a part of God's forever family.

CHARACTERS

JAMIE JAMISON – former intern who becomes a serious reporter

SCOOP BLAKELY – former intern in charge of coffee who becomes a goofy news reporter

PRODUCER – in charge of running the show, commercial breaks, etc.

SERVER – waiter or waitress from Mr. Zironi's

COSTUMES

JAMIE JAMISON – Slacks, Button-down shirt, Tie

SCOOP BLAKELY – Slacks, Button-down shirt, Tie

PRODUCER – All black clothing with headset and clipboard

SERVER – White button down shirt, Apron

SET

JUMP News Room – News desk, Two chairs, Camera

Mr. Zironi's Italian Restaurant – Rome decorations, Table, Chairs, Place setting

PROPS

Skit - Cue cards, Clipboard, Coffee cups, Papers/pencils for desk, Microphone, Pizza box, Fake money, Spaghetti

Lesson - Sandbags, Sturdy bag to drag the sandbags, Nice robe, 2 Volunteers (1 Father, 1 Son), "Father God" name tag, "Me" name tag

JUMP NEWS

LEADER DEVOTION

The prodigal son wanted independence and distance from his loving father. He wanted to live his life his way, apart from his father's influence. Asking his father for his share of his inheritance was akin to saying, "I wish you were dead, so I can have the money from your will." Can you imagine the hurt after hearing a loved son insinuate his life would be better if you were dead? This first step away from his father began the son's downfall. Any step away from our Heavenly Father will begin our downfall, if we are not quick to return to Him.

Before we start to judge the young man in Jesus' story, how many times do we commit the sin of self-sufficiency? How often do we choose to live under our own power and for our own initiatives rather than fully rely on our loving Heavenly Father to care for us and guide us?

Next the son chose to live a hedonistic life, one with no thought of the future. He used his father's money to buy friends and fun. At first his future looked bright - a new life full of independent freedom - until he realized his independence from his father was a dangerous pathway to his own destruction. Sin is deceptive. What at first looks beautiful, fun, and full of life reveals itself to be a trap that enslaves us and leads us to death.

Feeding pigs was an especially low state for a Jew, because pigs were considered unclean animals. Brought low by the consequences of his choices, the prodigal son came to his senses and started his journey home. When the father saw his son from a distance, he RAN to meet him. Because the father in this story represents God, this is the only time in the Bible we see God RUN. The father shows mercy when he forgives his son and grace when he reinstates him into the family, throwing a huge party for him.

Unfortunately, the father's other son missed the party. He allowed his pride to keep him from the joy of his father. Though he stood outside and pouted, the party continued without him.

We have all chosen to walk away from our Father God. We have all sinned. Aren't you glad we have a Heavenly Father who runs to us when we come to our senses, realizing our wrongs? He runs to each and every sinner who makes the choice to come home. He runs with forgiveness, mercy, grace, acceptance, and adoption. He celebrates His children's return from death to life. Don't miss the party.

PRE-SERVICE

Play fun music and videos as kids come into JUMP Worship. Skit characters Jamie and Scoop hold up various cue cards ("Applause," "Laugh," "Oooh," "Ahhh," "Oh no," etc.) during the music and videos, encouraging kids to participate.

COUNTDOWN VIDEO

JUMP Worship is starting! Lead the congregation in counting down. Worshiping together is fun, and we are ready to begin!

SONG

Lead the congregation in a fun worship song.

MAIN POINT VIDEO

WELCOME

Welcome to JUMP, where we worship God together! Does anyone remember what book of the Bible we are studying during our series, JUMP News? *(Luke)* Yes! Great job! We are studying Luke's collection of eye-witness accounts of Jesus' time on earth. We hear a lot of news stories every day, but in JUMP News we are learning about the greatest news of all time. Jesus is the best news the world has ever received! We should all tell the world about Jesus.

Our Main Point is "Jesus Forgives Sinners Like Me." The Bible says we have all sinned. We have all made wrong choices and deserve the punishment for those choices. Thankfully, Jesus loves us very much. He made a way for us to be a part of God's forever family. Jesus forgives sinners like you and like me. That is Good News!

Let's make motions to help us remember our Main Point. (*Make motions for the Main Point. Have kids repeat the motions and Main Point with you.*)

Now turn to your neighbor and say, "Hellooooo!" (*Hellooooo!*)
Turn to your other neighbor and say, "Sup, yo?" (*Sup, yo?*)
Tell them your name. Introduce yourself. (*Kids introduce themselves.*)
Now say "Jesus Forgives Sinners Like Me." (*Jesus Forgives Sinners Like Me.*)
Turn to the person behind you and say, "Hello to the back of your head!" (*Hello to the back of your head!*)
"Jesus Forgives Sinners Like Me." (*Jesus Forgives Sinners Like Me.*)
One last time, face me and say, "Jesus Forgives Sinners Like Me." (*Jesus Forgives Sinners Like Me.*)

Great job! I can't wait to open the Bible and learn more about this as we worship today. We have a few rules to help us worship the Lord, to keep our focus on Him and Him alone. Rule number one is STAY QUIET. When someone is up here talking, we should all be listening. Some people can talk and hear at the same time. Hearing me is not why we are here in JUMP. God has something to say to you, and we want to listen to Him. We want to pay attention with our heads and our hearts as we worship God today. Show me what that should look and sound like. (*Wait for kids to be quiet.*) Great job! Listening will help us stay focused on God.

Our second rule is KEEP YOUR HANDS AND FEET TO YOURSELF. Focusing on God is very difficult when the people around you are messing with you. Don't distract the people around you from worshiping God! Keep your hands and feet to yourself.

Rule number three is STAND UP DURING SONGS. JUMP is not a show. We are here to worship God together, so be a part of what we are doing. Think about the words of the songs when you sing. Use your hands and feet to worship God, not to mess with your friends.

And finally, our fourth rule is – say it with me – HAVE FUN! We are going to have so much fun today! Now let's worship God by talking to Him in prayer. Bow your heads and close your eyes. Focus on God only as we talk to Him in prayer.

PRAY

Lead the congregation in prayer.

JUMP SKIT PART 1

See skit script beginning on page 86.

LESSON 5 SKIT
PART 1
THE PRODIGAL SON

JESUS FORGIVES SINNERS LIKE ME.

Skit Intro Video

Welcome to JUMP NEWS with your news team: Weather with Wendy Storm, Traffic with Iona Ford, Sports with Will Wynn, Politics with Cam Pain, and news anchors, Justin Report and Johnny Onthespot.

SFX: NEWS TRANSITION MUSIC

JAMIE: Welcome back to JUMP NEWS! I'm Jamie Jamison, your JUMP NEWS reporter. Here to bring you the latest-breaking news that will pull at your heart strings and make your mind go, "Wow! That's some interesting news."

Producer holds up "Applause" sign.

JAMIE: My co-anchor should be joining me at any moment ... *Looks around for him.*

Scoop runs on with multiple coffees and sits at the desk.

SCOOP: AND WE'RE BACK! No worries, I got everyone's coffee order - just doing my job. Um ... *Looking at the coffee cup.* This one is for Iona Ford ... Iona! Order Up! Hello?

JAMIE: *Stays in news anchor voice.* Scoop, we're live.

SCOOP: *Still sorting out coffee cups on the anchor desk.* This one's for Cam Pain ... Cam!!

JAMIE: You're a reporter now. There's no need to get coffee for anyone.

SCOOP: This one's for Scoop. Who's Scoop? Oh, I'm Scoop! *Takes a drink and spits it out.* Yowza! This is disgusting. This must be yesterday's coffee.

JAMIE: All the people you got coffee for are on vacation. Remember? And if that's yesterday's coffee, then why were you late?

SCOOP: And we're back!

JAMIE: Scoop, we are live right now.

SCOOP: You're right! I've never felt so alive!

JAMIE: No. We are on the air.

SCOOP: Living on cloud nine, baby!!!!

JAMIE: Millions of people are seeing you right now.

SCOOP: *Suddenly bright eyed and scared.* Umm ... I'M SCOOP, HERE TO BRING YOU THE LATEST SCOOP!

JAMIE: Thank you, Scoop. Now for breaking news.   SFX: BREAKING NEWS   This just in: Our local soccer team, the Jumpin' Kickers, has made it to the Earth Cup!

SCOOP: NO WAY!

Producer holds up "Oooh" sign.

JAMIE: They will be facing off against none other than the fiercest team in the league ... Team Fluffy Bunnies. They are fierce!

Producer holds up "Ahhh" sign.

SCOOP: SERIOUSLY?! NO WAY!

JAMIE: Our very own Scoop has been following the team's progress for years as a devoted fan. Scoop, how excited are you for this match?

SCOOP: I am more excited than a bear that has just found a fresh hive of honey! If only I could be there to witness the majestic Jumpin' Kickers in action ... WOW! That would be AMAZING! Every time I think about the Jumpin' Kickers I ... AAAAAAAAHHHHHHHH!!!! Scream.

PRODUCER: And we're out in 3, 2, 1 ... Scoop, what happened to you out there??

SCOOP: I'm sorry. I just got so excited. I can't believe the Jumpin' Kickers are going to be in the finals and I'm not going to be able to go.

PRODUCER: Well, we have some good news for you, Scoop.

SCOOP: You do?

PRODUCER: We are going …

SCOOP: Yeah?

PRODUCER: To …

SCOOP: YEAH?!

PRODUCER: Send you …

SCOOP: YEAH?!

PRODUCER: All the way to …

SCOOP: NO WAY!!!!

PRODUCER: The parking lot!

SCOOP: Yeah! No Way! Huh?!

PRODUCER: To clean my car!

SCOOP: Oh … okay.

PRODUCER: Then when you finish … You're going to Italy!

SCOOP: NO WAY! THIS IS THE BEST DAY OF MY LIFE!!! AAAAAAAAAAAAAAHHHHHH!!!!
I'M SO HAPPY!

PRODUCER: And we're back in 3 … 2 … 1 …

Producer holds up "Applause" sign.

JAMIE: And we're back! I'm Jamie Jamison

SCOOP: And I'm the happiest person on earth! WOOHOO! I'm going to Italy!

JAMIE: OKAY … MORE BREAKING NEWS!   SFX: BREAKING NEWS   This just in. The Jumpin'
Kickers have added a new player to their team. Rumor has it that this player has the
strongest leg in the entire world. One man said he saw him kick a soccer ball through a
brick wall. This is really going to be a good thing for the Jumpin' Kickers. We are sending
our very own Scoop Blakely out into the field to cover this story.

SCOOP: I am so excited! This is going to be amazing!

JAMIE: We need you out in the field, reporting live from Italy. You better get going!

SCOOP: Right! *Frantic.* This is Live Blakely, reporting Scoop!

JAMIE: We'll be back after this commercial break.

Producer holds up "Applause" sign.

PRODUCER: And go to commercial in 3, 2, 1 … And we're out. Scoop, you are going to be on the first flight to Italy. I am going to give you $200 for this trip. Just to be clear, this money is for your ticket to the big game. DO NOT USE THIS MONEY ON ANYTHING ELSE.

SCOOP: But there are so many amazing things in Italy!

PRODUCER: Scoop! This money does not belong to you. You are going to Italy to report on the match. Now get going.

SCOOP: OK! I won't let you down!!

SFX: NEWS TRANSITION MUSIC

Scoop, Producer, and Jamie exit in opposite directions.

SONG *Lead the congregation in a fun worship song.*

SPECIAL REPORT
FROM THE BIBLE

JUMP NEWS

BIBLE LESSON INTRO VIDEO

 ### INTRO

Have you ever done something bad and didn't know what to do next? Maybe you decided to throw a ball inside and accidentally broke a lamp. Now you're just sitting there with the broken lamp panicking over what is going to happen when your parents get home. What do you do? Why in the world did you start throwing the ball inside? You knew you weren't supposed to, but it seemed like a good idea at the time. And now? Now you KNOW it was a bad idea. You just sit there staring at the broken lamp thinking, "Mom and Dad are gonna KILL me!"

At this point, you have another choice to make. Do you try to fix it yourself, trying to glue the lamp back together, or hide the pieces somewhere? Or do you tell your parents the truth? If you could go back in time and choose not to throw the ball in the house, you absolutely would, but that is, unfortunately, not an option. You've made the wrong choice, and now you have to choose what to do next.

Does that sound familiar to anyone? You may not have broken a lamp, but we all have made wrong choices. We all have chosen to sin. What are we going to do now? Jesus told an amazing parable, or story, in **Luke 15:11-32** to help us understand what God does when we choose to come to Him for forgiveness. Jesus' story is called the Parable of the Prodigal Son.

 ### READ THE BIBLE

In Jesus' story, a father had two sons. The younger son asked his father for all of the money he was supposed to inherit when his father died. Can you imagine telling your parents you wish they were dead, so you could have their money? The younger son was not making a good choice. The father gave his son the money, and the son left.

He spent all his money on himself. He lived a wild life until he was out of money. The prodigal son had made wrong choices.

To make a bad situation worse, there was a famine in the land. The younger son did not have any money. He did not have any food. He took the only job he could find, feeding pigs. He was so hungry he wished he could eat the pigs' food. He had made wrong choices. He had sinned against his father. He had done things he knew were wrong. What was he going to do now?

Read Luke 15:17-19.

The prodigal son "came to his senses." He decided to go back home to his father. He knew after all he had done, he did not deserve to be treated like family. He hoped his father would let him be a servant. At least that way, he would have something to eat.

Read Luke 15:20-24.

The father was so excited to see his son, that he ran to meet him. The father forgave his younger son and welcomed him back into the family. He threw a giant party, because his son had decided to come back home.

 # OBJECT LESSON

We are just like the prodigal son in this story. We have sinned: made choices that go against God.

Have two volunteers come on stage. Choose one to wear the "Father God" name tag and one to wear the "Me" name tag. Give "Me" a sturdy bag. Have the two start out together on stage right. Give several examples of sin (stealing, cheating, disobeying parents, having a bad attitude, saying unkind words, etc.) Each time you give an example of sin, have "Me" take a few steps away from "God" and place a sandbag in his bag. When "Me" gets to the end of the stage, have them pause.

Sin separates us from God and weighs us down. Though sin might look good at the time, it always leads to death and destruction. It takes us away from our Father God who loves us. Like the prodigal son, we have a choice to make. We can keep going farther and farther away from God. We can try to deal with our sin on our own. Or, like the prodigal son, we can come to our senses and head home. We can turn back to God. Look what happens when we turn to God asking Him to forgive us for our sins.

"Me" turns around toward "Father God" and says "I'm sorry". "Father God" runs across the stage to "Me", takes the bag, and gives "Me" a robe. "Father God" says, "Welcome home! You are family." The two exit, stage right, leaving the bag behind.

God runs to us when we turn to Him. He welcomes us into His family - God's family! He forgives us of our sins.

APPLICATION

So what do we do when we realize we are in big trouble? What do we do when we realize we have sinned?

1 John 1:9 says, "But if we confess our sins to him, he is faithful and just to forgive us our sins and to cleanse us from all wickedness."

Tell God you are sorry for the wrong things you have done. Tell Him you believe Jesus died on the cross to take the punishment for your sins. Tell God you believe Jesus came back to life three days later. Then choose to put Jesus in charge of your life from now on. Make Him the Lord, the Boss, of your life.

Turn to God, and He will run to you with open arms. Aren't you glad Jesus forgives sinners like you and me?

PRAY

OFFERING SONG

Lead the congregation in a slower worship song.

JUMP SKIT PART 2

See skit script beginning on page 93.

JESUS FORGIVES
SINNERS LIKE ME.

LESSON 5 SKIT
PART 2
THE PRODIGAL SON

JESUS FORGIVES SINNERS LIKE ME.

Skit Intro Video

Welcome to JUMP NEWS with your news team: Weather with Wendy Storm, Traffic with Iona Ford, Sports with Will Wynn, Politics with Cam Pain, and news anchors, Justin Report and Johnny Onthespot.

SFX: NEWS TRANSITION MUSIC

JAMIE: We're back with JUMP NEWS. I'm Jamie Jamison, and we're proud to bring you live coverage from the Earth Cup!

Producer holds up "Applause" sign.

JAMIE: We've got our reporter, Scoop, out in the field. What's the scoop, Scoop?

Lights up on Scoop standing next to a server that is holding a pizza box.

SCOOP: Hey, Jamie! You'll never believe where I am?

JAMIE: I'm guessing you're at the Earth Cup in Italy, if I'm not mistaken?

SCOOP: Nope! I'm at Mr. Zironi's Italian Restaurant, about to eat 6 double-decker pizzas and set the world record for most pizzas ever eaten by a single human being!

JAMIE: What was that, Scoop? It sounded like you said you are about to eat 6 double-decker pizzas. But that just cannot be correct. Scoop, you're supposed to be at the Earth Cup covering the game!

SCOOP: And I will be, right after I eat these pizzas! Here I go! In three, two, one! *Doesn't even open pizza box.* I can't! I ate two footlong meatball subs before I came here!

JAMIE: Scoop, why would you eat before an eating contest?

SCOOP: I couldn't help myself!

SERVER: It's going to be $70.

SCOOP: That's okay, I've got $200 to spend right here!

JAMIE: Scoop, you're supposed to be using that money to cover the game!

SCOOP: Here you go sir, and here's another $30 for your trouble! Alright, I'm Scoop, and that's the scoop!

PRODUCER: What's he doing!? He's going to run out of money before he even covers the game! Those tickets to the game are $200. He already doesn't have enough money now to get into the game!

JAMIE: *Aside.* I'm sure Scoop has a plan sir. *Back to the camera.* Thanks, Scoop! We were hoping to hear some news about the game. Any news for the eager viewers?

SCOOP: Hey Jamie, I'm about to eat the largest plate of spaghetti in all of Italy. It's been my dream to conquer the world's greatest meat-uh-balls! Alright, here I go!

JAMIE: Wait, Scoop, you can't possibly be trying another eating challenge right now. You just failed the last one. You couldn't even take one bite!

SCOOP: That's all in the past, Jamie! You have to live in the now! That's how Scoop lives it! Alright, here I go, in 3, 2, 1 ... I can't do it! I'm still full from those two subs I downed earlier. Why do I keep doing this?

SERVER: That'll be $50.

SCOOP: No problem, here's another fifty for your trouble!

JAMIE: Wait, Scoop, that's all your money! How are you going to get into the game?

SCOOP: Where there's a will, there's a way. Next time you see me will be at the Earth Cup!

JAMIE: Alright, good luck, Scoop. Don't go anywhere, we'll be right back with coverage of the Cup!

Video: Commercial

PRODUCER: I don't know how he's going to get into this game. He has no money!

JAMIE: We'll see...

PRODUCER: Alright, we're back in 3, 2, 1 ...

JAMIE: Welcome back to JUMP NEWS

Producer holds up "Applause" sign.

JAMIE: Join us as we go live now to Scoop at the Earth Cup!

Nobody there.

JAMIE: Uh … Scoop, are you there? Um… Well, it looks like we've lost Scoop. I don't know where he is! *Aside.* Cut to commercial!

PRODUCER: We can't! We just got back from commercial!

JAMIE: *Frantic.* We'll be right back!

PRODUCER: No, we won't!

JAMIE: *Aside.* Where is Scoop?

PRODUCER: I don't know!

JAMIE: *Aside.* It doesn't look like he ever made it to the Cup! *To the camera.* Bear with us just a moment as we are experiencing technical difficulties. *Aside.* I hope he's okay! He's in Italy with no money!

Scoop enters.

SCOOP: Hey everyone …

They scream.

JAMIE: Scoop, you're here!

SCOOP: I know, I know! I didn't make it to the Cup. I ran out of money. I'm going to get fired, I just know it.

JAMIE: Scoop, we're just glad you're okay.

SCOOP: This is the end for me! Take me away, where I'll never see daylight again. I don't deserve to read the news for such a great station. The world's greatest local news channel that only reports to kids. I'm sorry!! Lock me up!! Take me away! I don't deserve this!!

JAMIE: Scoop, just calm down!

PRODUCER: Scoop, you're back!

SCOOP: I know, I'm fired! I'll pack up my stuff and go!

PRODUCER: Scoop, you're not fired. We're just glad you're okay!

SCOOP: I'm not fired?

PRODUCER: No, I've spent the last hour calling everyone in Italy trying to find you. I'm just glad you're okay!

Producer holds up "Awww" sign.

SCOOP: Yah, but I spent all your money, and I didn't even get the story.

PRODUCER: That's okay, Scoop. Everyone makes mistakes. This reminds me of the special report we heard today about the Prodigal Son. Even though the Prodigal Son took his father's money and spent it all, his father still welcomed him with open arms when he returned. The same way he forgave his son and Jesus forgives us, I choose to forgive you. Now come on, we've got some news to report!

JAMIE: Wait a second, Scoop. How'd you get back from Italy so fast?

SCOOP: It didn't take very long to get back. I was just in little Italy down the street.

JAMIE: What? Scoop, the Earth Cup was happening in the country Italy...

SCOOP: Yowzah!!

Producer holds up "Laugh" sign.

JAMIE: C'mon Scoop, let's go grab some pizza!

SCOOP: But, I already ate two subs...

JAMIE: This is Jamie Jamison and Scoop Blakely signing off. Remember, when life hands you lemons, check for mold.

SFX: NEWS TRANSITION MUSIC

SONG *Lead the congregation in a fun worship song.*

MEMORY VERSE VIDEO

MEMORY VERSE

Our memory verse is from the book of Luke, chapter four, verses eighteen and nineteen. These verses are about Jesus!

Read the verses with me. **Luke 4:18-19 "The Spirit of the LORD is upon me, for he has anointed me to bring Good News to the poor. He has sent me to proclaim that captives will be released, that the blind will see, that the oppressed will be set free, and that the time of the LORD's favor has come."**

The Good News is that Jesus made a way for us to have a right relationship with God. We are just like the prodigal son. I'm glad God loves us so much He sent His Son, Jesus, to take the punishment for our sins. Because of Jesus, we can be a part of God's forever family. Jesus is the best news the world has ever received! Let's review the motions to the first part of this verse.

Repeat after me.
Luke 4:18-19 *(Luke 4:18-19)*
"The Spirit of the LORD is upon me *(The Spirit of the LORD is upon me)*,
for he has anointed me to bring *(for he has anointed me to bring)*
Good News to the poor *(Good News to the poor)*.
He has sent me to proclaim *(He has sent me to proclaim)*
that captives will be released *(that captives will be released)*,
that the blind will see *(that the blind will see)* ... "

Great job! Stand up and let's say everything we have learned together, starting with "Luke 4:18-19" on the count of three. One, two, three: **Luke 4:18-19 "The Spirit of the LORD is upon me, for he has anointed me to bring Good News to the poor. He has sent me to proclaim that captives will be released, that the blind will see ... "**

Now let's see if we can say the verse without looking at the screens.

Take the verse off the screens.

One, two, three: **Luke 4:18-19 "The Spirit of the LORD is upon me, for he has anointed me to bring Good News to the poor. He has sent me to proclaim that captives will be released, that the blind will see ... "**

Great job! Jesus is the best news the world has ever received! I challenge you to tell someone the Good News about Jesus this week.

ANNOUNCEMENTS

Use this time to encourage kids to bring friends and participate in whatever you may have coming up next.

REVIEW GAME

It's time for the REVIEW GAME!! I need one volunteer from each grade to come up on stage. I will choose people who have been listening and paying attention the whole service and want to play in our game.

Choose contestants and introduce them to the group in game show style.

During this game, your grade can win by getting very quiet when you hear the wrong answer and very loud when you hear the right answer. Each grade is going to have a different silly move and sound that you must do when you think you hear the right answer. (*Let your contestants choose a silly motion and sound for their grade.*)

I hope you are ready. I hope you have been paying attention, because the game begins ... NOW!

Give kids the opportunity to do their motions and silly sounds when they hear the correct answer. Award points to the grade who is the quietest when they hear the wrong answer and participates the most when they hear the right answer.

Question 1: What was today's Main Point?
    a. Jesus Forgives Sinners Like You.
    b. Jesus Forgives Sinners Like Me.
    c. Don't Run Away From Home.
    d. When Life Hands You Lemons, Check for Mold.

Question 2: Where can you find today's Bible lesson?
    a. Matthew 15:11-32
    b. Mark 15:11-32
    c. Luke 15:11-32
    d. Luke 2

Question 3: What did the prodigal son do with his father's money?

    a. ate 6 double-decker pizzas   c. gave it to charity

    b. wasted it on wild living   d. bought chickens

For added fun, play "The Chicken Dance" each time you read a wrong answer about chickens. Act bewildered, like you do not know where the music is coming from. Read the question again and continue.

Question 4: What happened when he finally decided to come home?

    a. His father kicked him out.   **c. His father ran to him, made him**

    b. His father made him a servant.   **part of the family, and threw a party.**

     d. His father did the chicken dance.

Question 5: In Luke 15, _____ are like the prodigal son, and _____ is like the father.

    a. all of us, God   c. only bad people, God

    b. my brother, my pet iguana   d. only good people, Farmer Joe's chicken

Question 6: Luke 4:18 says, "He has sent me to proclaim that captives will be released, that the _____ will _____ ..."

    a. blind, see   c. seeing, go blind

    b. free people, be put in jail   d. tacos, be served on Tuesdays

SONG

Lead the congregation in a fun worship song.

DISMISSAL

JESUS IS THE

BEST

NEWS THE
WORLD HAS
EVER RECEIVED

LESSON 6

BIBLE LESSON

THE RICH YOUNG RULER
Luke 18:18–30

MAIN POINT

JESUS IS MORE IMPORTANT THAN ANYTHING ELSE.

MEMORY VERSE

LUKE 4:18–19 "The Spirit of the Lord is upon me, for he has anointed me to bring Good News to the poor. He has sent me to proclaim that captives will be released, that the blind will see, that the oppressed will be set free, and that the time of the Lord's favor has come."

LESSON 6
HIGHLIGHTS

SPIRITUAL CONNECTION

Jamie and Scoop have the opportunity to interview a famous basketball player, Kareem-Abdul J'Bryant. J'Bryant gives Scoop an autographed t-shirt, and Scoop loses sight of what is really important. Instead of focusing on J'Bryant, Scoop focuses on J'Bryant's gift. The rich young ruler from Luke 18:18-30 also focused more on the gift than the Gift Giver. Sadly, he focused more on his money than on Jesus. We should remember that Jesus is more important than anything else, including the many gifts He has given us.

CHARACTERS

JAMIE JAMISON – former intern who becomes a serious reporter

SCOOP BLAKELY – former intern in charge of coffee who becomes a goofy news reporter

PRODUCER – in charge of running the show, commercial breaks, etc.

KAREEM-ABDUL J'BRYANT – famous basketball player

COSTUMES

JAMIE JAMISON – Slacks, Button-down shirt, Tie

SCOOP BLAKELY – Slacks, Button-down shirt, Tie

PRODUCER – All black clothing with headset and clipboard

KAREEM-ABDUL J'BRYANT – Basketball jersey

SET

JUMP News Room – News desk, Two chairs, Camera

PROPS

Skit - Cue cards, Clipboard, Coffee cups, Papers/pencils for desk, Microphone, Donut box, Basketball, Autographed t-shirt

Lesson - Plastic pearl necklace, Paper strips for everyone, Pencils for everyone

JUMP NEWS

LEADER DEVOTION

READ LUKE 18:18-30

The young man in Luke 18 was most likely a "ruler" of a synagogue. Some scholars believe he held a seat in the Jewish Council or Sanhedrin. Though he was bold enough to go respectfully to Jesus without any pretext or trickery, the young man's question was flawed. He asked what he must do to earn eternal life, implying he thought he was in good standing with the Law at this point in his life. He was unable to see the sin in his heart.

Jesus answered the man by listing commandments five through nine. These commandments teach us how to love others. So far, so good! To his knowledge, the man had not broken any of those commandments. But Jesus, the Light of the World, knew his heart and illuminated the problem. What did the man love more: his possessions or his God, his social status or his status with the Almighty? As Jesus said in **Luke 16:13, "No one can serve two masters. For you will hate one and love the other; you will be devoted to one and despise the other. You cannot serve God and be enslaved to money."** Unfortunately, the rich young ruler chose to enjoy the pleasures of this world rather than to store up his treasures in Heaven.

The more blessed with worldly things we are in this life, the harder it will be for us to realize our need to abandon ourselves to our Savior. While receiving His blessings on this earth is not wrong, worshiping His blessings is. Thankfully, nothing is impossible with God. The God who created our hearts can certainly change them, if we are willing to follow Him (Luke 19:1-10).

Jesus affirms Peter's decision to leave behind his family, his job, and his earthly securities to follow Him. Jesus assures Peter he will receive everything he left behind and more in Heaven. God does not want us to be without blessings. He wants us to be without idols. **Isaiah 44:6 says, "This is what the Lord says—Israel's King and Redeemer, the Lord of Heaven's Armies: 'I am the First and the Last; there is no other God.'"**

Ask the Lord to search your heart and show you what you need to surrender to Him. Ask Him to reveal any idols or any areas of pride in your life. Commit to put Him first, to give Him priority in your heart. Reaffirm that He alone is your God and thank Him for being a Light to your heart as you grow in your relationship with Him.

PRE-SERVICE

Play fun music and videos as kids come into JUMP Worship. Skit characters Jamie and Scoop hold up various cue cards ("Applause," "Laugh," "Oooh," "Ahhh," "Oh no," etc.) during the music and videos, encouraging kids to participate.

COUNTDOWN VIDEO

JUMP Worship is starting! Lead the congregation in counting down. Worshiping together is fun, and we are ready to begin!

SONG

Lead the congregation in a fun worship song.

MAIN POINT VIDEO

WELCOME

Welcome to JUMP, where we worship God together! Does anyone remember what book of the Bible we are studying during our series, JUMP News? (Luke) Yes! Great job! We are studying Luke's collection of eye-witness accounts of Jesus' time on earth. We hear a lot of news stories every day, but in JUMP News we are learning about the greatest news of all time. Jesus is the best news the world has ever received! We should all tell the world about Jesus.

Our Main Point is "Jesus Is More Important than Anything Else."

Let's make motions to help us remember our Main Point. (Make motions for the Main Point. Have kids repeat the motions and Main Point with you.)

Now turn to your neighbor and say, "Hello!" (Hello!)
"How are you?" (How are you?)

Tell them how you are. Now turn to your other neighbor and say, "HELLOOO!" *(HELLOOO!)*

Now say "YOU are important!" *(YOU are important!)*

"I am important!" *(I am important!)*

"But Jesus Is More Important than Anything Else." *(But Jesus Is More Important than Anything Else.)*

Point to *(volunteer's name)* and say "YOU ROCK!" *(YOU ROCK!)*

"Did you know Jesus Is More Important than Anything Else?" *(Did you know Jesus Is More Important than Anything Else?)*

"Because He is!" *(Because He is!)*

One last time, face me and say, "Jesus Is More Important than Anything Else." *(Jesus Is More Important than Anything Else.)*

Jesus really is more important than anything else. No person and no thing will ever be as important as Jesus. I can't wait to open the Bible and learn more about this as we worship today. We have a few rules to help us worship the Lord, to keep our focus on Him and Him alone. Rule number one is STAY QUIET. When someone is up here talking, we should all be listening. Some people can talk and hear at the same time. Hearing me is not why we are here in JUMP. God has something to say to you, and we want to listen to Him. We want to pay attention with our heads and our hearts as we worship God today. Show me what that should look and sound like. *(Wait for kids to be quiet.)* Great job! Listening will help us stay focused on God.

Our second rule is KEEP YOUR HANDS AND FEET TO YOURSELF. Focusing on God is very difficult when the people around you are messing with you. Don't distract the people around you from worshiping God. Keep your hands and feet to yourself.

Rule number three is STAND UP DURING SONGS. JUMP is not a show. We are here to worship God together, so be a part of what we are doing. Think about the words of the songs when you sing. Use your hands and feet to worship God, not to mess with your friends. After all, nothing is more important than Jesus!

And finally, our fourth rule is – say it with me – HAVE FUN! We are going to have so much fun today! Now let's worship God by talking to Him in prayer. Bow your heads and close your eyes. Focus on God only as we talk to Him in prayer.

PRAY

Lead the congregation in prayer.

JUMP SKIT PART 1

See skit script beginning on page 106.

LESSON 6 SKIT
PART 1
THE RICH YOUNG RULER

JESUS IS MORE IMPORTANT THAN ANYTHING ELSE.

Skit Intro Video

Welcome to JUMP NEWS with your news team: Weather with Wendy Storm, Traffic with Iona Ford, Sports with Will Wynn, Politics with Cam Pain, and news anchors, Justin Report and Johnny Onthespot.

SFX: NEWS TRANSITION MUSIC

JAMIE: Welcome back to JUMP NEWS! I'm Jamie Jamison, your JUMP NEWS reporter. Here to bring you the latest-breaking news that will pull at your heart strings and make your mind go, "Wow! That's some interesting news."

Producer holds up "Applause" sign.

JAMIE: Please welcome my co-anchor, Scoop Blakely!

Producer holds up "Applause" sign. Scoop runs on with multiple coffees and sits at the desk.

SCOOP: AND WE'RE BACK! No worries, I got everyone's donut order - just doing my job. *Looking at the box.* Will Wynn …Will? Will Wynn, I have your donuts here.

JAMIE: You're a reporter now, Scoop. How many times do I have to tell you this? There's no need to get coffee or breakfast for anyone. All the people you got food for are on vacation. Remember?

SCOOP: And we're back!

JAMIE: Scoop, we are live right now.

SCOOP: You're right - I've never felt so alive! I'M SCOOP, HERE TO BRING YOU THE LATEST SCOOP!

JAMIE: Thank you, Scoop. Now for breaking news. **SFX: BREAKING NEWS** This just in: Our very own home town sports legend Kareem-Abdul J'Bryant will be stopping by the studio for an exclusive interview with our very own Scoop Blakely!

Producer holds up "Oh My" sign.

SCOOP: What? You're talking about the greatest sports legend in the history of our city! Maybe I can get his autograph, maybe even take a selfie with him. Maybe I'll get him to autograph the selfie! This is going to be great! AAAAAAAAAAHHHHHHHHHH!!!!

JAMIE: You heard it here, first! Kareem-Abdul J'Bryant live in the studio after these messages.

SCOOP: AAAAAAAAAAHHHHHHHHHHHH!!!!

Producer holds up "Applause" sign.

PRODUCER: And we're out in 3, 2, 1 ... Scoop, what happened to you out there??

SCOOP: I'm sorry. I just get so excited. THE J'Bryant is coming to our station! This is crazy! I've watched every single one of his games since preschool. I even found clips of him when he was playing ball during recess.

PRODUCER: Well, that's a little creepy Scoop, but we need you to be professional. You get to ask him 10 questions, so you've got to figure out exactly what questions you're going to ask. Do you think you can handle this?

SCOOP: Oh, definitely! But I can only ask 10 questions?! I don't know how I'll ever narrow it down to only 10. There are so many things I want to ask!

PRODUCER: Well make sure you keep it simple, okay! He's going to be here any moment, and when he gets here I don't want you to lose focus.

SCOOP: I won't lose focus. I just CAN'T BELIEVE HE'S COMING HERE! I've got so many things to ask!

PRODUCER: See, Scoop, you just lost focus. Why don't you go compose yourself and think about what questions you're going to ask Mr. J'Bryant when he gets here.

SCOOP: No problem. Don't worry, I'll get the Scoop!

SFX: NEWS TRANSITION MUSIC

Scoop, Producer, and Jamie exit.

SONG   *Lead the congregation in a fun worship song.*

SPECIAL REPORT
FROM THE BIBLE

JUMP NEWS

BIBLE LESSON INTRO VIDEO

 INTRO

Once upon a time, there was a little girl who loved her plastic pearl necklace. The necklace was made out of plastic and only painted to look like pearls, but the little girl loved how nice the necklace looked on her. She wore it to school, to play, and even tried to wear it to bed. Of course, her father would not let her wear the pearl necklace to bed, because it was a choking hazard. So every night, the little girl would sadly take off her pearl necklace and put it in a very special box.

One night, as the father was tucking her into bed, he looked at his daughter and said, "Will you give me your pearl necklace?" The young girl hugged the pearl necklace in the special box and said, "No, daddy, no. I love my pearl necklace. I want to keep it." With a sad look on his face, the father finished putting his daughter to bed and left. The next night, the father asked his daughter again, "Will you give me your pearl necklace?" Again, the daughter said no. Night after night, the father asked, and night after night, the young girl refused to let go of her plastic pearl necklace.

It's hard to give up the things we love, the things that are important to us, isn't it? In Luke 18, Jesus helped a rich young ruler realize what was really most important to him. Though he said he loved God more than anything else, the truth was he loved money more.

 READ THE BIBLE

One day, the rich young ruler came to ask Jesus how he could earn eternal life. Now we know that no one can earn eternal life, because we all have sinned. We have broken God's rules in one way or another, and we need Jesus. This young man, though, could not see he had ever done anything wrong.

Jesus pointed out that the young man had followed many of the commandments. He was very good at loving others. Then Jesus showed the young man his problem: he loved something else more than God.

Read Luke 18:22-23.

The rich young ruler loved his money more than he loved God. He was not willing to give up his wealth to follow Jesus, so he left very sad.

Read Luke 18:24-25.

In other words, it is very difficult for some people with many blessings to put God first.

James 1:17 says, "Whatever is good and perfect is a gift coming down to us from God our Father, who created all the lights in the heavens. He never changes or casts a shifting shadow."

It is not wrong to have money, but it is wrong to love your money, your things, more than you love God. God has given many people wealth as His gift to them, but He does not want them to worship the gift. He wants us to worship Him, not what He gives us.

God has given each of us wonderful gifts. He has given us family, friends, money, sports, art, music, and much more. Many of those things are important to us, and that's great. It is good that your family is important to you. It is good that playing sports is important to you. The problem comes when any of these gifts becomes more important to us than the God who gave them to us. God does not ask everyone to give away all of the gifts He has given them. But He does ask us to be willing to let them go in order to follow Him. God deserves first place in our hearts.

Read Luke 18:26-27.

Just because it is difficult does not mean it is impossible. Nothing is impossible with God. In fact, next week, we will learn about a rich young man who did choose to give up his wealth in order to follow Jesus.

 ## APPLICATION

The little girl from our earlier story loved her plastic pearl necklace so much, but she saw how sad her father was every time she refused to give the pearls to him. Finally, one night, the father came to tuck the little girl in and asked again, "Will you give me your pearl necklace?" With tears in her eyes, the little girl slowly handed her father her pearl necklace. She did not want her father to be sad. She decided she loved her father more than she loved her necklace, so she gave him the necklace. The father smiled, said, "Thank you," and left the room.

A few minutes later, the father returned with a small velvet box and handed it to his little girl. Confused, the girl opened the box to find a brand new necklace made of real pearls.

Read Luke 18:28–30.

The choice to make Jesus the most important thing in our lives is not all about giving everything away. It's about choosing something better. The girl had to let go of her plastic pearls, so she could have real pearls instead.

Are you holding on to a gift God has given you instead of holding on to God Himself? Jesus is more important than anything else. He is more important than sports. He is more important than being popular. He is more important than making good grades. Jesus is more important than money.

Have volunteers pass out strips of paper. As we go into our time of offering, we are going to pass out strips of paper and pencils. During the offering song, very quietly write down on this paper something important to you that you are willing to give to Jesus. Then, quietly drop that paper into the offering plate as a symbol of giving it to God, reminding yourself that only God deserves first place in your life.

PRAY

OFFERING SONG

Lead the congregation in a slower worship song.

JUMP SKIT PART 2

See skit script beginning on page 111.

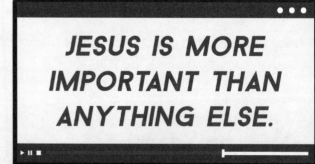

JESUS IS MORE IMPORTANT THAN ANYTHING ELSE.

JUMP NEWS

JESUS IS MORE IMPORTANT THAN ANYTHING ELSE.

Skit Intro Video

Welcome to JUMP NEWS with your news team: Weather with Wendy Storm, Traffic with Iona Ford, Sports with Will Wynn, Politics with Cam Pain, and news anchors, Justin Report and Johnny Onthespot.

SFX: NEWS TRANSITION MUSIC

JAMIE: We're back with JUMP News, I'm Jamie Jamison.

Producer holds up "Applause" sign.

JAMIE: We're proud to bring you an exclusive interview right here in our studio with Kareem-Abdul J'Bryant by our field reporter, Scoop Blakely. Give us the scoop, Scoop.

SCOOP: No problem. I'd like to welcome to the studio, Mr. Kareem-Abdul J'Bryant!

J'Bryant enters, carrying a basketball.

SCOOP: *Girlish Scream.* Ahhhhh!!!!!! It's Kareem-Abdul J'Bryant! This is unreal! He's here to see me! Scoop! The greatest sports reporter of all time. Standing 5'7", out of the University of Guadalupe, number one sports reporter! *Scooooooop Blaaaaaaaaaaaakley!!!!! Scoop steals the ball from him and starts to dribble.*

JAMIE: Okay, Scoop keep it together!

SCOOP: You're right! Hi, Mr. J'Bryant, it's so nice to meet you! *Starts shaking his hand and won't let go.* I'm your biggest fan. I've got all your trading cards and all your jerseys, and one time I collected your dirty socks out of a trash can after a game ...

J'BRYANT: That's great, glad to hear it ...

SCOOP: *Still shaking his hand.* And another time, I was watching you on TV, and when I yelled your name, you looked right at me! Did you hear me? I bet you did, cuz I was really screaming your name ...

J'BRYANT: That's great …

SCOOP: I mean it was really loud. It sounded just like this … *Yelling.* "J'BRYANT! What are you doing? You've got to hit your free-throws! J'BRYANT it's not a one man show! There's no "I" in team! Get yourself together man! You're the best!

J'BRYANT: Well I appreciate that … I think. I want to thank you guys for having me on the show. They told me you were a big fan, Scoop. So, I brought you a little gift. It's an autographed t-shirt from yours truly, Señor J'Bryant.

SCOOP: *Girlish scream.* Ahhh!!! *Faints and then quickly gets back up.* No way! I don't know how to thank you! It's the greatest gift I've ever gotten. I can't wait to keep looking at it forever!

J'BRYANT: No problem. Are you ready for this interview?

SCOOP: Yeah, yeah, yeah … Sure, but first, how do I look with the shirt on!? *Puts shirt on.*

JAMIE: Shirt looks great, Scoop, but we're running out of time. You'd better get to your questions.

SCOOP: Right! Alright, Mr. J'Bryant, question number one! When you get on the court, and you know you need to hit the big shot, and everyone is counting on you … What do you think of how I look in this shirt!?

J'BRYANT: Oh … Uh … I think the shirt looks great.

SCOOP: No way! Alright, next question … When you wake up on gameday, and you know you've got to eat a breakfast for champions, how do you think this shirt looks in the back?

J'BRYANT: Uh, it looks fine.

SCOOP: Not too tight or too lose? Okay thanks! Okay, question #3. You've got a lot of good teammates … Now, if you had to guess which one of them would like this shirt the most, which would it be?

J'BRYANT: Um, I'm not sure.

SCOOP: Did you say shirt?

J'BRYANT: No, I said sure …

SCOOP: Oh, it sounded like you said shirt! I thought maybe you were saying how nice my shirt is.

JAMIE: Scoop, I think you're getting a little off track. Here, take this basketball and pass it back and forth with Mr. J'Bryant. Maybe that will help you clear your head!

SCOOP: Yah sure, sounds good!

Gets basketball and starts passing it back and forth with J'Bryant.

SCOOP: Alright! Here we go. Wow, you're a great passer! Have you ever passed the ball to someone wearing a shirt this nice?

J'BRYANT: We usually play in jerseys.

SCOOP: That's too bad. Just look at this shirt!

Scoop looks down to admire his shirt and gets hit in the face with ball and is knocked down.

JAMIE: Scoop, you okay!?

SCOOP: I'm good!

JAMIE: Oh, that's all the time we have today with our special guest. Thank you so much for joining us, Kareem-Abdul J'Bryant. I'm Jamie Jamison and that was Scoop Blakely signing off. Remember, when life hands you lemons, check for mold.

Producer holds up "Applause" sign. J'Bryant exits.

SCOOP: Man, that interview went really well!

JAMIE: You didn't ask a single question that didn't have to do with your shirt.

SCOOP: Well, I don't know if you saw it, but it's a really nice shirt.

JAMIE: You were so focused on the shirt he gave you, you didn't focus on J'Bryant at all. I'm starting to think you care more about that shirt than you do J'Bryant, and he's the one who gave it to you! You know Scoop, this reminds me of the special report we heard today about the Rich Young Ruler. He was so focused on all of his money, he forgot that God was the one who gave it to him in the first place.

SCOOP: Oh, wow. I hadn't even realized ... I've been more focused on the gift than the person who gave it to me. I think I owe him an apology.

JAMIE: Well, I think he's in the snack room.

SCOOP: Alright, first I'm gonna apologize, and then I'm gonna get the interview we all came here for!

JAMIE: There we go! Go get em' Scoop!

Scoop exits, dribbling the ball and accidentally hits his foot and runs after the ball off-stage.

SFX: NEWS TRANSITION MUSIC

SONG *Lead the congregation in a fun worship song.*

MEMORY VERSE VIDEO

MEMORY VERSE

Our memory verse is from the book of Luke, chapter four, verses eighteen and nineteen. These verses are about Jesus!

Read the verses with me. **Luke 4:18-19 "The Spirit of the LORD is upon me, for he has anointed me to bring Good News to the poor. He has sent me to proclaim that captives will be released, that the blind will see, that the oppressed will be set free, and that the time of the LORD's favor has come."**

The Good News is that Jesus made a way for us to have a right relationship with God. We are just like the prodigal son. I'm glad God loves us so much He sent His Son, Jesus, to take the punishment for our sins. Because of Jesus, we can be a part of God's forever family. Jesus is the best news the world has ever received! Let's review the motions to what we have learned so far.

Repeat after me.
Luke 4:18-19 *(Luke 4:18-19)*
"The Spirit of the LORD is upon me *(The Spirit of the LORD is upon me)*,
for he has anointed me to bring *(for he has anointed me to bring)*
Good News to the poor *(Good News to the poor)*.
He has sent me to proclaim *(He has sent me to proclaim)*
that captives will be released *(that captives will be released)*,
that the blind will see *(that the blind will see)* ... "

Great job! Let's make motions for the next part of this verse. *(Make motions for the key words and phrases in the next part of the verse. Use these motions each time you say the verse.)*

Repeat after me:
"that the oppressed *(that the oppressed)*
will be set free *(will be set free)* ...

An oppressed person is someone who is treated harshly and unfairly. Jesus came, so we could all be free from our slavery to sin. Because of Jesus, we can have a right relationship with God and share His forever home in heaven.

Stand up and let's say everything we have learned together, starting with "Luke 4:18-19" on the count of three. One, two, three: **Luke 4:18-19 "The Spirit of the LORD is upon me, for he has anointed me to bring Good News to the poor. He has sent me to proclaim that captives will be released, that the blind will see, that the oppressed will be set free … "**

Now let's see if we can say the verse without looking at the screens.

Take the verse off the screens.

One, two, three: **Luke 4:18-19 "The Spirit of the LORD is upon me, for he has anointed me to bring Good News to the poor. He has sent me to proclaim that captives will be released, that the blind will see, that the oppressed will be set free … "**

Great job! Jesus is the best news the world has ever received! I challenge you to tell someone the Good News about Jesus this week.

ANNOUNCEMENTS

Use this time to encourage kids to bring friends and participate in whatever you may have coming up next.

REVIEW GAME

It's time for the REVIEW GAME!! I need one volunteer from each grade to come up on stage. I will choose people who have been listening and paying attention the whole service and want to play in our game.

Choose contestants and introduce them to the group in game show style.

During this game, your grade can win by getting very quiet when you hear the wrong answer and very loud when you hear the right answer. Each grade is going to have a different silly move and sound that you must do when you think you hear the right answer. (*Let your contestants choose a silly motion and sound for their grade.*)

I hope you are ready. I hope you have been paying attention, because the game begins … NOW!

Give kids the opportunity to do their motions and silly sounds when they hear the correct answer. Award points to the grade who is the quietest when they hear the wrong answer and participates the most when they hear the right answer.

Question 1: What was today's Main Point?

a. Jesus Is More Important than Most Things.

b. Jesus Is More Important than Some Things.

c. Jesus Is More Important than Anything Else.

d. When Life Hands You Lemons, Check for Mold.

Question 2: Where can you find today's Bible lesson?

a. Matthew 18:18-30

b. Luke 18:18-30

c. Leviticus 18:18-30

d. Luke 2

Question 3: What did Jesus tell the rich young ruler to do?

a. Sell all his possessions, give the money to the poor, and follow Him.

b. Sell all his possessions and use the money to build a house.

c. Give away his possessions and live under a bridge.

d. Sell all his possessions and buy chickens.

For added fun, play "The Chicken Dance" each time you read a wrong answer about chickens. Act bewildered, like you do not know where the music is coming from. Read the question again and continue.

Question 4: Why was the rich young ruler sad?

a. He loved his money more than Jesus.

b. He saw a sad animal commercial.

c. He did not understand.

d. His father did the chicken dance.

Question 5: Is anything impossible for God?

a. Yes. Some things are impossible.

b. No! Nothing is impossible for God.

c. I don't know.

d. Did someone say... chicken?

Question 6: Luke 4:18-19 says, "He has sent me to proclaim that captives will be released, that the blind will see, that the _____ will be set _____ ..."

a. wrong, right

b. free people, in jail

c. oppressed, free

d. tacos, on my plate

SONG

Lead the congregation in a fun worship song.

DISMISSAL

REPORTING
LIVE
FROM THE
BOOK OF LUKE

LESSON 7

BIBLE LESSON

ZACCHAEUS
Luke 19:1-10

MAIN POINT

JESUS CHANGES HEARTS.

MEMORY VERSE

LUKE 4:18-19 "The Spirit of the Lord is upon me, for he has anointed me to bring Good News to the poor. He has sent me to proclaim that captives will be released, that the blind will see, that the oppressed will be set free, and that the time of the Lord's favor has come."

LESSON 7
HIGHLIGHTS

SPIRITUAL CONNECTION

Jamie and Scoop interview a notorious donut robber, closely mirroring the story of Zacchaeus in Luke 19. After talking with Scoop, the donut robber learns the error of his ways and decides to give back all the donuts he stole and more. When Zacchaeus met Jesus, he changed his ways and offered to pay everyone back four times the amount he had stolen.

CHARACTERS

JAMIE JAMISON – former intern who becomes a serious reporter

SCOOP BLAKELY – former intern in charge of coffee who becomes a goofy news reporter

PRODUCER – in charge of running the show, commercial breaks, etc.

DONUT ROBBER – constantly robs the donut shop on 6th Street

COSTUMES

JAMIE JAMISON – Slacks, Button-down shirt, Tie

SCOOP BLAKELY – Slacks, Button-down shirt, Tie

PRODUCER – All black clothing with headset and clipboard

DONUT ROBBER – Mask, Black and white striped t-shirt, Black pants, Black gloves

SET

JUMP News Room - News desk, Two chairs, Camera

6th Street - Park bench, Potted plants

PROPS

Skit - Cue cards, Clipboard, Coffee cups, Papers/pencils for desk, Microphone, To-go cartons, Donut box

Lesson - 2 Posters (labeled "Jesus" and "Me"), Yarn (to attach the poster around the neck), 2 Volunteers ("Jesus" and "Me"), Sin cards, Fruit of the Spirit cards, Tape

JUMP NEWS

LEADER DEVOTION

READ LUKE 19:1-10

Zacchaeus was living proof that Jesus changes hearts. Zacchaeus was a dishonest, Jewish tax collector for the Roman government. By his countrymen, he was seen as a traitor. In fact, the Jews had disowned him. Because he was not a Roman by birth, the Romans probably would not have held Zacchaeus in high esteem either. By those who knew him personally, he was seen as a thief. By Jesus, Zacchaeus was seen for who he was: a lost soul in desperate need of a Savior.

Despite the "grumbles" of the people, Jesus invited Himself to Zacchaeus' house. We may never know what Jesus said to Zacchaeus at dinner to ignite such a radical change in his behavior. What we do know is that Jesus changes the hearts of those who are willing to give up everything to follow Him. Unlike the rich young ruler, Zacchaeus was willing to let go of his money in order to make amends with everyone he had cheated. Most likely, this was everyone in the town where he collected taxes. Repaying everyone four times the amount he had taken probably bankrupted Zacchaeus of his earthly treasures.

Zacchaeus' encounter with Jesus changed his identity. Jesus called Zacchaeus a "son of Abraham" to affirm his place in the Jewish community. He had been rejected, but in Christ, he was accepted. He had been unloved, but in Christ, he was greatly loved. He had been alone, but in Christ, he had a Friend and a forever family. He had been lost, but now in Christ, he was found.

Do you believe Jesus changes hearts? Have you allowed Him to change your heart? Zacchaeus let go of his pride, climbing a tree to see the Savior as He passed by. Let go of your pride. Admit you are poor in spirit, that you cannot earn His favor on your own merit. Ask Him to search your heart for sins that are building a wall in your relationship with God. Ask Him to change you from the inside out, because you believe He can. And, like Zacchaeus, gladly let go of the things that hold you in bondage.

Luke shows us again and again that Jesus has come **"to seek and save those who are lost." (Luke 19:10)** Take time today to celebrate those who have been found by Jesus. Accept those whom Christ has accepted, and forgive those whom Christ has forgiven. Jesus changes hearts. Now that's Good News!

PRE-SERVICE

Play fun music and videos as kids come into JUMP Worship. Skit characters Jamie and Scoop hold up various cue cards ("Applause," "Laugh," "Oooh," "Ahhh," "Oh no," etc.) during the music and videos, encouraging kids to participate.

COUNTDOWN VIDEO

JUMP Worship is starting! Lead the congregation in counting down. Worshiping together is fun, and we are ready to begin!

SONG

Lead the congregation in a fun worship song.

MAIN POINT VIDEO

WELCOME

Welcome to JUMP, where we worship God together! Does anyone remember what book of the Bible we are studying during our series, JUMP News? *(Luke)* Yes! Great job! We are studying Luke's collection of eye-witness accounts of Jesus' time on earth. We hear a lot of news stories every day, but in JUMP News we are learning about the greatest news of all time. Jesus is the best news the world has ever received! We should all tell the world about Jesus.

Our Main Point is "Jesus Changes Hearts."

Let's make motions to help us remember our Main Point. *(Make motions for the Main Point. Have kids repeat the motions and Main Point with you.)*

Now turn to your neighbor and say, "Hi!" (*Hi!*)
"How are you?" (*How are you?*)
Tell them how you are. Now turn to your other neighbor and say, "Hello!" (*Hello!*)
Introduce yourself. (*Kids introduce themselves.*)
Now say "You can change your favorite color." (*You can change your favorite color.*)
"You can change your clothes." (*You can change your clothes.*)
"But only Jesus changes hearts." (*But only Jesus changes hearts.*)
Turn back to your other neighbor and say "Jesus Changes Hearts!" (*Jesus Changes Hearts!*)
One last time, face me and say, "Jesus Changes Hearts!" (*Jesus Changes Hearts!*)

Nothing is impossible for Jesus. He changes hearts every day. I know He has changed mine. I can't wait to open the Bible and learn more about this as we worship today. We have a few rules to help us worship the Lord, to keep our focus on Him and Him alone. Rule number one is STAY QUIET. When someone is up here talking, we should all be listening. Some people can talk and hear at the same time. *Hearing* me is not why we are here in JUMP. God has something to say to you, and we want to *listen* to Him. We want to pay attention with our heads and our hearts as we worship God today. Show me what that should look and sound like. (*Wait for kids to be quiet.*) Great job! Listening will help us stay focused on God.

Our second rule is KEEP YOUR HANDS AND FEET TO YOURSELF. Focusing on God is very difficult when the people around you are messing with you. Don't distract the people around you from worshiping God. Keep your hands and feet to yourself.

Rule number three is STAND UP DURING SONGS. JUMP is not a show. We are here to worship God together, so be a part of what we are doing. Think about the words of the songs when you sing.

And finally, our fourth rule is – say it with me – HAVE FUN! We are going to have so much fun today! Now let's worship God by talking to Him in prayer. Bow your heads and close your eyes. Focus on God only as we talk to Him in prayer.

PRAY

Lead the congregation in prayer.

JUMP SKIT PART 1

See skit script beginning on page 124.

LESSON 7 SKIT
PART 1

ZACCHAEUS

JESUS CHANGES HEARTS.

Skit Intro Video

Welcome to JUMP NEWS with your news team: Weather with Wendy Storm, Traffic with Iona Ford, Sports with Will Wynn, Politics with Cam Pain, and news anchors, Justin Report and Johnny Onthespot.

SFX: NEWS TRANSITION MUSIC

JAMIE: Well, hello there! I'm Jamie Jamison, your JUMP NEWS reporter. Here to bring you the latest-breaking news that will pull at your heart strings and make your mind go, "Wow! That's some interesting news."

Producer holds up "Applause" sign.

JAMIE: And now, please welcome my co-anchor, Scoop Blakely.

Scoop runs on with multiple containers and sits at the desk.

SCOOP: AND WE'RE BACK! No worries, I got everyone's egg orders ready. I've been up all-night cooking everyone's eggs. Just doing my job. *Looking at the box.* This one is for Wendy. Wendy Storm, sunny side up, that's how you like 'em right? Order Up! Hello?

JAMIE: *Stays in news anchor voice.* Scoop, we're live.

SCOOP: *Still sorting out containers on the anchor desk.* We got scrambled for Iona Ford, you like 'em scrambled, right?!

JAMIE: You're a reporter now. How many times do I have to tell you this. There's no need to get breakfast for anyone. All the people you got food for are on vacation. Remember? Scoop, we are live right now.

SCOOP: You're right, Jamie. I've never felt so alive! Living on cloud nine! Probably because I ate 8 eggs this morning … And it looks like I have a lot more to eat now. A LOT. *Snapping out of it.* I'M SCOOP, HERE TO BRING YOU THE LATEST SCOOP!

JAMIE: Thank you, Scoop. Now for Breaking News! `SFX: BREAKING NEWS` The Donut Robber of 6th Street strikes again. Notorious for robbing donut stores located on 6th Street, the thief was seen robbing another donut store and has been caught! He is willing to do an interview about his crime, but he's stated that he will only allow the interview to be done if it's with our very own Scoop Blakely.

SCOOP: What? No! Are you talking about THE Donut Robber of 6th Street? I don't want to do an interview with him. He's scary, and he steals donuts! I love donuts, and I would never steal them. Do I have to interview him? I won't, I cant! Every time I think about donuts being stolen I just want to scream!

JAMIE: WOAH! I'm going to stop you right there, Scoop. I know you may not want to, but he'll only do the interview with you. And don't worry, he's not dangerous. He just loves to steal donuts. You can handle this!

SCOOP: Alright, I can do this! I might just give him a piece of my mind. From one donut lover to another, he "DONUT" realize what he's doing wrong. Haha. See what I did there? Donut? Get it?

Producer holds up "Laugh" sign.

SCOOP: Thank you. I'll be here all week. I think … Back to you, Jamie.

JAMIE: Our very own Scoop has agreed to interview the Donut Robber of 6th Street, so don't go anywhere. We'll be right back!

`SFX: NEWS TRANSITION MUSIC`

Jamie and Scoop exit in opposite directions.

`SONG` *Lead the congregation in a fun worship song.*

SPECIAL REPORT

FROM THE BIBLE

BIBLE LESSON INTRO VIDEO

 INTRO

Jesus is the best news the world has ever received. For the last several weeks, we have learned about Jesus from the book of Luke. Jesus taught us how to love others the way God loves us. Jesus also did amazing miracles. He healed the sick, walked on water, calmed the storm, and even raised people from the dead. Jesus also changed hearts. You may not think of that as a miracle, but it absolutely is. Only God can forgive sins and change people's hearts for Him.

In Luke 18, we learned Jesus offered a rich young ruler the chance to change. He offered the man a chance to leave everything behind and follow Him. Unfortunately, the man loved his money more than God. He decided not to follow Jesus.

Today's Bible story has a much happier ending. A rich man named Zacchaeus decided to follow Jesus; to give Jesus first place, and Jesus miraculously changed his heart.

 READ THE BIBLE

Luke 19 tells us Jesus was passing through Jericho. Everywhere Jesus went, large crowds of people followed Him. People wanted to see Jesus do miracles, hear Him teach, and ask Him for help. The streets were very crowded when Jesus was passing by. Zacchaeus was too short to see Jesus, and no one would let him through to see.

No one liked Zacchaeus, because he was a Jew who collected taxes for the Roman government. The Roman government had taken over Israel, and the Israelites were not happy about it. Roman soldiers would often force Jews to let them stay in their houses, and they were often not good house guests. The Romans could even force the Jews to carry their heavy gear for at least a mile. If the Israelites were going to pay taxes, they would rather pay their own government, not the Romans.

Because Zacchaeus collected taxes for the Romans, the people in Jericho saw him as a traitor. On top of that, Zacchaeus often told the people they owed more taxes than they really did. He lied to them, so that he could keep the extra money for himself. The people knew Zacchaeus was stealing from them, but there was nothing they could do about it. He worked for the Roman government, and the Roman government allowed him to steal from the people in this way.

Knowing this, I'm not sure I would have liked Zacchaeus either! When Zacchaeus realized he was not going to be able to see Jesus over the crowds of people, he climbed a sycamore tree.

Read Luke 19:5-6.

Out of all the people lined up to see Him, Jesus picked Zacchaeus' house to visit. Zacchaeus?! Why wouldn't Jesus pick someone who worked in the synagogue or someone who was kind to others? Why on earth did Jesus pick a bad guy like Zacchaeus? The people started to mumble.

Then something amazing happened. Jesus changed Zacchaeus' heart. We may never know what happened that made Zacchaeus completely change the way he did, but he changed from a greedy and selfish person to one who was willing to give everything away to follow Jesus.

Read Luke 19:8-10.

 # APPLICATION + OBJECT LESSON

Jesus came "to seek and to save what was lost." Zacchaeus had lost his way in life. He was not living the way God designed us to live.

Bring one of your two volunteers onto the stage. Have this volunteer put the "Me" poster around their neck.

Zacchaeus lied and stole from the people. *Tape two "sin" signs on the "Me" poster.*

We all have sinned, too. Maybe you chose not to obey all of your parents' instructions. *Tape a "sin" sign on the "Me" poster.*

Or maybe you cheated on a test. You didn't get caught, but that wrong choice still stains your heart. *Tape a "sin" sign on the "Me" poster.*

Maybe you said unkind words to a brother or sister. Or maybe you said the right words, but you said them in a very mean way. *Tape a "sin" sign on the "Me" poster.*

Maybe you were really angry at your brother or sister, so you hit them. *Tape a "sin" sign on the "Me" poster.*

Each time we sin, it stains our hearts. It keeps us from having a friendship with God.

Thankfully, Jesus changes hearts. When we ask Jesus to forgive us of our sins, He does. He takes all our sin and wipes it away.

Bring your second volunteer onto the stage. Have this volunteer wear the "Jesus" poster around their neck. As you speak, have "Jesus" remove the "sin" signs from "Me" and throw them away.

Only Jesus can do something that amazing. Then with Jesus as our Boss, we get to spend time with Him, getting to know Him. And as we get to know Him, Jesus changes our hearts.

As you speak, have "Jesus" tape the Fruit of the Spirit signs onto "Me".

He does so much more than just take away sin. Jesus also builds good things into our hearts like love, joy, peace, patience, kindness, goodness, faithfulness, gentleness, and self control.

Have you asked Jesus to change your heart?

PRAY

OFFERING SONG

Lead the congregation in a slower worship song.

JUMP SKIT PART 2

See skit script beginning on page 129.

JESUS CHANGES HEARTS.

JUMP NEWS

LESSON 7 SKIT
PART 2
ZACCHAEUS

JESUS CHANGES HEARTS.

Skit Intro Video

Welcome to JUMP NEWS with your news team: Weather with Wendy Storm, Traffic with Iona Ford, Sports with Will Wynn, Politics with Cam Pain, and news anchors, Justin Report and Johnny Onthespot.

SFX: NEWS TRANSITION MUSIC

JAMIE: We're back with JUMP NEWS, I'm Jamie Jamison.

Producer holds up "Applause" sign.

JAMIE: We're excited to bring you an exclusive interview with The Donut Robber of 6th Street by our very own Scoop Blakely. Give us the scoop, Scoop!

Lights up on Scoop standing next to the Donut Robber and holding a box of donuts.

SCOOP: I'm here on the scene with the Donut Robber, and just let me start by asking why would you do it?

ROBBER: I love donuts!

SCOOP: Well me too, but I'm not going to steal them.

ROBBER: Then you must not love donuts as much as I do!

Scoop gasps.

ROBBER: I would do anything for a warm donut.

SCOOP: But ... I don't think you realize what you are doing to the ...

ROBBER: *Interrupting.* One time I wanted a donut so bad, I dressed as a giant donut and hid in the store every day until the employees would leave. Once everyone was gone, I jumped out of my costume and ate all the donuts. The next morning, they wondered what happened to the donuts, and I was already back in my donut suit. The only reason they caught me was because I got so hungry one night, I ate my donut costume.

SCOOP: Was it made of real donuts?

ROBBER: No! But it looked delicious. I didn't care! My love for donuts took over and I had to eat it!

Producer holds up "Oh My" sign.

SCOOP: It doesn't matter how much you like donuts. Stealing them is wrong!

ROBBER: You must not really like donuts!

SCOOP: Yes, I do!

ROBBER: No, you don't!

SCOOP: I do too!

ROBBER: I don't think so!

SCOOP: Yes!

ROBBER: No!

SCOOP: YES!

ROBBER: NO!

SCOOP: NO!

ROBBER: YES!

SCOOP: GOTCHA!!

ROBBER: Wait, what?! A real donut lover would understand why I steal donuts!

SCOOP: Oh Yeah! Let me tell you a story about a real donut lover. I would wake up every morning, brush my teeth with jelly, rinse my hair with donut glaze, and when I blew my nose, sprinkles came out. Because all I did was think about donuts. I mowed every person's yard that I could see. There was only one house on my block, so it wasn't that bad ... but it was a big house. They would pay $10 dollars, which was a lot of money back in 1923.

ROBBER: Wait, how old are you? You were alive in 1923?

SCOOP: That's not important! I would take every dime that I had and save up for donuts. I once saved up so much money, I had a donut themed birthday party! It was amazing!! It was at that party, I shared my very first donut with my best friend, Don. *To the camera.* Sorry, Jamie.

JAMIE: No worries.

SCOOP: Don was the only person who enjoyed donuts as much as I did.

ROBBER: What did you say that boy's name was?

SCOOP: First name Don … Last name Oteater. Don Oteater! He enjoyed donuts too much to steal them like you.

ROBBER: Scoop, I have something to tell you.

SCOOP: What?!

ROBBER: It's me...

SCOOP: I know. You're the Donut Robber of 6th Street.

ROBBER: No … It's me … Don!

He takes off his mask.

SCOOP: Don would never!

ROBBER: I know, I lost my way.

SCOOP: How could you, Don? Don't you realize what you're doing? If you steal all of the donuts from 6th Street without paying for them, then the Donut Shop of 6th street will go out of business.

ROBBER: OH …

SCOOP: Then nobody will be able to have any donuts.

ROBBER: OH NO!

SCOOP: People have to have their donuts. Plus, it is just wrong to steal! You have to stop this.

ROBBER: You're right. I don't how I got here. I feel terrible. I'm so sorry.

SCOOP: It's okay.

ROBBER: You know what … I am going to open my own donut shop.

SCOOP: Yeah?

ROBBER: And I'm not going to make anyone pay for the donuts in my shop. FREE DONUTS FOR EVERYONE!

SCOOP: That's great!

ROBBER: I'm going to give back all the donuts I've stolen and more!

SCOOP: That's the Don Oteater that I know!

ROBBER: Thanks for your help, Scoop.

SCOOP: My pleasure, Don!

They hug. Producer holds up "Awww" sign.

SCOOP: Back to you, Jamie. My second-best friend.

JAMIE: Wow! *Emotional.* I can honestly say that was the best news report I have ever seen. Scoop, you really have become an amazing reporter.

SCOOP: *Shows up on set way too fast.* Thanks, Jamie! You are pretty good yourself.

JAMIE: Wow, that was really fast.

SCOOP: Well, we are only on 5th Street.

JAMIE: Right. Well, that's all for today, folks. This is Jamie Jamison, signing off.

SCOOP: And I'm Scoop Blakely.

JAMIE: Say it with us!

JAMIE/SCOOP: When life gives you lemons … Check for mold!

SFX: NEWS TRANSITION MUSIC

SONG   *Lead the congregation in a fun worship song.*

MEMORY VERSE VIDEO

MEMORY VERSE

Our memory verse is from the book of Luke, chapter four, verses eighteen and nineteen. These verses are about Jesus!

Read the verses with me. **Luke 4:18-19 "The Spirit of the LORD is upon me, for he has anointed me to bring Good News to the poor. He has sent me to proclaim that captives will be released, that the blind will see, that the oppressed will be set free, and that the time of the LORD's favor has come."**

The Good News is that Jesus made a way for us to have a right relationship with God. We are just like the prodigal son. I'm glad God loves us so much He sent His Son, Jesus, to take the punishment for our sins. Because of Jesus, we can be a part of God's forever family. Jesus is the best news the world has ever received! Let's review the motions to what we have learned so far.

Repeat after me.
Luke 4:18-19 *(Luke 4:18-19)*
"The Spirit of the LORD is upon me *(The Spirit of the LORD is upon me)*,
for he has anointed me to bring *(for he has anointed me to bring)*
Good News to the poor *(Good News to the poor)*.
He has sent me to proclaim *(He has sent me to proclaim)*
that captives will be released *(that captives will be released)*,
that the blind will see *(that the blind will see)*
that the oppressed will be set free *(that the oppressed will be set free)* ... "

Great job! Let's make motions for the last part of this verse. *(Make motions for the key words and phrases in the last part of the verse. Use these motions each time you say the verse.)*

Repeat after me:
" ... and that the time *(and that the time)*
of the LORD's favor *(of the LORD's favor)*
has come *(has come)*."

Jesus was telling everyone He is God's promised Savior. When we choose to believe in Him, to make Him the Boss of our lives, Jesus will change our hearts forever. That is Good News!

Stand up and let's say both verses together, starting with "Luke 4:18-19" on the count of three. One, two, three: **Luke 4:18-19 "The Spirit of the LORD is upon me, for he has anointed me to bring Good News to the poor. He has sent me to proclaim that captives will be released, that the blind will see, that the oppressed will be set free, and that the time of the LORD's favor has come."**

Now let's see if we can say the verse without looking at the screens.

Take the verse off the screens.

One, two, three: **Luke 4:18-19 "The Spirit of the LORD is upon me, for he has anointed me to bring Good News to the poor. He has sent me to proclaim that captives will be released, that the blind will see, that the oppressed will be set free, and that the time of the LORD's favor has come."**

You are amazing! I am so proud of you. Remember, Jesus is the best news the world has ever received! I challenge you to tell someone the Good News about Jesus this week.

ANNOUNCEMENTS

Use this time to encourage kids to bring friends and participate in whatever you may have coming up next.

REVIEW GAME

It's time for the REVIEW GAME!! I need one volunteer from each grade to come up on stage. I will choose people who have been listening and paying attention the whole service and want to play in our game.

Choose contestants and introduce them to the group in game show style.

During this game, your grade can win by getting very quiet when you hear the wrong answer and very loud when you hear the right answer. Each grade is going to have a different silly move and sound that you must do when you think you hear the right answer. (*Let your contestants choose a silly motion and sound for their grade.*)

I hope you are ready. I hope you have been paying attention, because the game begins ... NOW!

Give kids the opportunity to do their motions and silly sounds when they hear the correct answer. Award points to the grade who is the quietest when they hear the wrong answer and participates the most when they hear the right answer.

Question 1: What was today's Main Point?
    a. I Can Change Your Heart.
    b. Jesus Changes Hearts.
    c. You Can Change Your Heart.
    d. When Life Hands You Lemons, Check for Mold.

Question 2: Where can you find today's Bible lesson?
    a. Luke 19:1-10
    b. Zacchaeus 19:1-10
    c. Leviticus 19:1-10
    d. Luke 2

Question 3: Where did Jesus want to eat dinner in Luke 19?
    a. The mayor's house
    b. A Pharisee's house
    c. Zacchaeus' house
    d. A chicken coop.

For added fun, play "The Chicken Dance" each time you read a wrong answer about chickens. Act bewildered, like you do not know where the music is coming from. Read the question again and continue.

Question 4: Why were the people surprised Jesus chose Zacchaeus' house?
    a. Zacchaeus was not a good man.
    b. Zacchaeus' house was ugly.
    c. Zacchaeus did not have a house.
    d. Zacchaeus was bad at the chicken dance.

Question 5: Is anything impossible for God?
    a. Yes. Some things are impossible.
    b. No! Nothing is impossible for God.
    c. I don't know.
    d. Did someone say... chicken?

Question 6: Luke 4:18-19 says, "He has sent me to proclaim that captives will be released, that the blind will see, that the oppressed will be set free, and that the time of the _____ _____ has come."
    a. remembering this verse
    b. dancing fever
    c. LORD's favor
    d. Taco Tuesday

SONG

Lead the congregation in a fun worship song.

DISMISSAL

JESUS IS THE

BEST

NEWS THE
WORLD HAS
EVER RECEIVED

LESSON 8

BIBLE LESSON

THE LAST SUPPER
Luke 22:14-23; 23:33-24:12

MAIN POINT

REMEMBER JESUS' SACRIFICE.

MEMORY VERSE

LUKE 4:18-19 "The Spirit of the Lord is upon me, for he has anointed me to bring Good News to the poor. He has sent me to proclaim that captives will be released, that the blind will see, that the oppressed will be set free, and that the time of the Lord's favor has come."

LESSON 8
HIGHLIGHTS

SPIRITUAL CONNECTION

Jamie and Scoop interview a retiring police chief, Chief Hector Ulysses Goneoutski. Chief Goneoutski encourages the citizens to remember the law and abide by it. In Luke 22, Jesus urges His disciples to remember His sacrifice. We can choose to remember Jesus' sacrifice by obeying Him out of love.

CHARACTERS

JAMIE JAMISON – former intern who becomes a serious reporter.

SCOOP BLAKELY – former intern in charge of coffee who becomes a goofy news reporter.

PRODUCER – in charge of running the show, commercial breaks, etc.

POLICE CHIEF – retiring hero

COSTUMES

JAMIE JAMISON – Slacks, Button-down shirt, Tie

SCOOP BLAKELY – Slacks, Button-down shirt, Tie

PRODUCER – All black clothing with headset and clipboard

POLICE CHIEF – Police costume, Badge

SET

JUMP News Room – News desk, Two chairs, Camera

Dinner – Table with bowl of punch, Food, etc.

PROPS

Skit - Cue cards, Clipboard, Snack food, Muffin, Papers/pencils for desk, Speech, Microphone, To-go cartons, Donut box

Lesson - None

LEADER DEVOTION

Technology has made it unnecessary to memorize many of the things people used to know by heart. Phone numbers, for example, used to be one of the most important things children memorized. High school students almost always knew the numbers of a few good friends. Today, smart phones keep all our information for us. We don't need to memorize anything except the processes needed to find the information we have stored on our devices.

But there is one thing Jesus asks us to remember - His sacrifice. At the Last Supper, Jesus broke bread to show the disciples that He, the Bread of Life, was about to be broken for their sins and the sins of the world. He drank wine to show that He, the Perfect Lamb, was about to pour out His blood as a final atonement for sin. Jesus made a commitment to carry out His Father's will, and He does not want us to forget.

Most of us would say we have never forgotten the story of Jesus' sacrifice and resurrection. Once you hear a story like that, it's hard to forget. But Jesus instituted the Lord's Supper, so His disciples would remember not just factually what happened, but also spiritually what happened. Jesus wants us to set aside time to remember in our hearts the consequences of our sins and the enormity of His love for us.

Take time right now to ask the Lord to examine your heart. Ask Him to reveal any sin in your heart that needs to be confessed. Then take time to remember Him. Make a list of all the times He has shown you His love, beginning with the cross to the present. Remember the times He has carried you through heartache. Remember the times He has blessed you beyond what you could imagine. Remember Him. Then, thank the Lord for His boundless love for you. Thank Him for His consistent and unconditional love for you.

Pray the kids in your class will get excited we serve a risen Savior! We remember what He has done and still get to marvel at what He is doing in this world today. We get to look forward to what He will do in the future, because He is risen!

LESSON 8 — JUMP NEWS

PRE-SERVICE

Play fun music and videos as kids come into JUMP Worship. Skit characters Jamie and Scoop hold up various cue cards ("Applause," "Laugh," "Oooh," "Ahhh," "Oh no," etc.) during the music and videos, encouraging kids to participate.

COUNTDOWN VIDEO

JUMP Worship is starting! Lead the congregation in counting down. Worshiping together is fun, and we are ready to begin!

SONG

Lead the congregation in a fun worship song.

MAIN POINT VIDEO

WELCOME

Welcome to JUMP, where we worship God together! This is the last lesson in our series, JUMP News. Does anyone remember what book of the Bible we are studying during our series, JUMP News? *(Luke)* Yes! Great job! We have been studying Luke's collection of eye-witness accounts of Jesus' time on earth. We hear a lot of news stories every day, but in JUMP News we are learning about the greatest news of all time. Jesus is the best news the world has ever received! We should all tell the world about Jesus.

Our Main Point is "Remember Jesus' Sacrifice."

Let's make motions to help us remember our Main Point. *(Make motions for the Main Point. Have kids repeat the motions and Main Point with you.)*

Now turn to your neighbor and say, "Hi!" *(Hi!)*
"How are you?" *(How are you?)*
Tell them how you are. Now turn to your other neighbor and say, "Hello!" *(Hello!)*
Introduce yourself. *(Kids introduce themselves.)*
Now say "Remember Jesus' Sacrifice." *(Remember Jesus' Sacrifice.)*
Turn back to your other neighbor and say "Remember Jesus' Sacrifice." *(Remember Jesus' Sacrifice.)*
One last time, face me and say, "Remember Jesus' Sacrifice." *(Remember Jesus' Sacrifice.)*

Jesus died on the cross, sacrificing His life, to pay the punishment we deserve for our wrong choices. He wants us to remember what He did and how much He loves us. I can't wait to open the Bible and learn more about this as we worship today. We have a few rules to help us worship the Lord, to keep our focus on Him and Him alone. Rule number one is STAY QUIET. When someone is up here talking, we should all be listening. Some people can talk and hear at the same time. Hearing me is not why we are here in JUMP. God has something to say to you, and we want to listen to Him. We want to pay attention with our heads and our hearts as we worship God today. Show me what that should look and sound like. *(Wait for kids to be quiet.)* Great job! Listening will help us stay focused on God.

Our second rule is KEEP YOUR HANDS AND FEET TO YOURSELF. Focusing on God is very difficult when the people around you are messing with you. Don't distract the people around you from worshiping God. Keep your hands and feet to yourself.

Rule number three is STAND UP DURING SONGS. JUMP is not a show. We are here to worship God together, so be a part of what we are doing. Think about the words of the songs when you sing.

And finally, our fourth rule is – say it with me – HAVE FUN! We are going to have so much fun today! Now let's worship God by talking to Him in prayer. Bow your heads and close your eyes. Focus on God only as we talk to Him in prayer.

PRAY

Lead the congregation in prayer.

JUMP SKIT PART 1

See skit script beginning on page 142.

LESSON 8 SKIT
PART 1

THE LAST SUPPER

REMEMBER JESUS' SACRIFICE.

Skit Intro Video

Welcome to JUMP NEWS with your news team: Weather with Wendy Storm, Traffic with Iona Ford, Sports with Will Wynn, Politics with Cam Pain, and news anchors, Justin Report and Johnny Onthespot.

SFX: NEWS TRANSITION MUSIC

JAMIE: Well, hello there! I'm Jamie Jamison, your JUMP NEWS reporter. Here to bring you the latest-breaking news that will pull at your heart strings and make your mind go, "Wow! That's some interesting news."

Producer holds up "Applause" sign.

JAMIE: I might be a temporary news reporter, while all the other anchors are out on vacation turning their skin into leather on a tropical island shore somewhere, but, as you know … *Dramatic pause.* I've always been a news anchor at heart. And now, over to my co-anchor … *Looks around, worried and whispers -* Scoop? Has anyone seen … Scoop?

SCOOP: *Scoop enters eating a muffin and interrupting Jamie while talking with his mouth full.* Have you seen all the food they have around here? I mean it is ridiculous. Each morning when I come into my temporary dressing room, there is a whole spread …

JAMIE: *Trying to get Scoop's attention.* Scoop, we are live.

SCOOP: *Not noticing the camera or lights.* You bet we're alive! We are LIVIN' LARGE! LIVIN' THE DREAM! Now this is the job I'm TALKIN' ABOUT!!!!! I used to have to get everyone's coffee and …

JAMIE: *Trying to get Scoop's attention.* Hey, Scoop.

SCOOP: *Continuing.* I was having to remember all kinds of crazy stuff! For example; like what time to come in to work, and how "Late Breaking News" didn't mean come in to work late and smash up whatever you want, while you are here … *Takes remainder of muffin and smashes it on the desk.*

JAMIE: *Still trying to get Scoop's attention.* Scoop! There is a camera right there, and this is really happening live.

SCOOP: What are you talking about? That doesn't even make any sense. If we were live on air, there would be a camera right there, you would have that crazy smile on your face that you get when the camera is on and thousands of people are … *Scoop realizes that Jamie has the "crazy" smile on his face, then slowly realizes that they are live on air.* Watching … our … every … move … *Snapping into reporting mode but speaking way too loudly.* HELLO, AND WELCOME BACK TO JUMP NEWS. I'M SCOOP BLAKELY HERE TO BRING YOU THE SCOOP!

JAMIE: *Interrupting.* Yes, we've already gone through that, and welcome back to reality! *Turning back to camera.* Let's get right to our breaking news story for today. SFX: BREAKING NEWS Today we have a fascinating story about a man that has sacrificed his entire life for others. Our entire community will be remembering and honoring the great deeds performed by none other than the Police Chief of Hock-A-Mookie Falls.

SCOOP: *With a loud disgusting sound, Scoop hocks a loogie on the ground.*

Producer holds up "Ewww" sign.

JAMIE: *Disgusted.* Might I remind you, Scoop, we are still on air! You cannot hock a loogie in the News Studio!!!!

SCOOP: *Confused.* I thought you just said to hock-a-loogie. So, I did!!! *Motions to the camera.* This is the news, you know! We are supposed to do what we say … obviously.

JAMIE: No! No! NO! I did not say, "hock-a-loogie," I said the name of our town, Hock-A-Mookie Falls.

SCOOP: *With a loud disgusting sound, Scoop hocks a loogie on the ground.*

Producer holds up "Ewww" sign.

JAMIE: *Blank Stare.* You say you made the coffee this morning?

SCOOP: Oh yeah! You betcha. Everyday.

JAMIE: *Slides coffee cup in front of him away.* Back to our story. Today we will have the privilege of going live to the Last Dinner in honor of Police Chief of Hock-A-Mookie Falls. *Scoop rears back as though to spit again, but Jamie stops him.* Don't even think about it! As we all know, the police chief will give his final remarks about his career, things he has taught his deputies, and also his desires for the future of the police department in his closing remarks tonight. What a privilege it will be to hear from such a wonderful leader, and brave man who has protected us from so much danger in his 33 years on the force.

SCOOP: Tune in tonight for the live coverage of the Police Chief's Last Dinner as ... Well, the Police Chief. And as always, if you're choosing a news channel to watch, make sure the news that is being reported is like a good cup of coffee; bold, strong and doesn't burn your mouth!

JAMIE: *Perplexed.* That made no sense. *Back to camera.* We'll be back after this commercial break.

SFX: NEWS TRANSITION MUSIC

Jamie and Scoop exit in opposite directions.

SONG *Lead the congregation in a fun worship song.*

SPECIAL REPORT
FROM THE BIBLE

JUMP NEWS

BIBLE LESSON INTRO VIDEO

 INTRO

How many of you like riddles? Listen very closely, and you may just be able to answer this one! You can't use a calculator, though, so listen closely.

> You are driving an east coast bus from Boston to Houston. Seventeen people get on the bus in Boston. In New York, six people get off the bus and nine people get on. In Roanoke, two people get off and four get on. In Birmingham, eleven people get off and sixteen people get on. In Laurel, three people get off and five people get on. In Baton Rouge, six people get off and three get on. You then arrive in Houston. What was the name of the bus driver?
>
> The bus driver was YOU, so the driver's name is YOUR name!

The answer to this riddle was the first detail I said. You probably remembered that detail right away when you heard the answer. It's not that you forgot what I said, or that you weren't listening. You probably just did not realize how important that first fact was. The first sentence was clouded in your memory by all of the other information in the riddle.

Our main point today is "Remember Jesus' Sacrifice." That may sound odd at first, because of course, we would not forget what Jesus did for us. But like in the riddle, although we may not forget the facts of what happened, we may sometimes forget how important Jesus' sacrifice was. We sometimes forget to honor Him in our hearts. Thankfully, Jesus knows us. He put a plan in place to help us remember His sacrifice during His last meal, before He was crucified.

READ THE BIBLE

Take a minute to remember how amazing Jesus' life on earth was. Jesus walked on water, healed the sick, and even brought dead people back to life! Jesus taught the people about God and showed everyone what it really meant to love others with God's love. Jesus knew He came to earth to take the punishment for our sins, and the punishment for sin is death. Throughout His ministry, Jesus warned the disciples He would one day choose to die, so everyone in the world could be forgiven for their wrong choices.

The night that Jesus was going to be arrested, He sat down to eat the Passover meal with His disciples. Remember, the Jews celebrate Passover to remember the amazing things God did to rescue the Israelites from slavery in Egypt. When Jesus started to speak to His disciples, He was reminding them once again, He was the Savior who was going to save the world from its slavery to sin.

Read Luke 22:19.

Jesus told the disciples to imagine the bread was His body, and then He broke the bread. Ouch! Jesus was about to be hurt very badly. He knew what was coming, and He did not want His disciples to forget His sacrifice.

Read Luke 22:20.

Jesus told the disciples to imagine the wine in the cup was His blood. He knew He was about to bleed a lot, and He did not want them to forget His sacrifice.

Christians all over the world still take the Lord's Supper to remember Jesus' sacrifice. They drink wine, or grape juice, and eat bread to remember everything Jesus did for them.

After the Passover dinner, Jesus went to the Garden of Gethsemane to pray. At the garden, Judas, one of His disciples, betrayed Jesus and brought Roman soldiers to arrest Him. Jesus did not fight the soldiers. In fact, He stopped Peter from fighting. Jesus went quietly.

Throughout the night, Jesus was sent from one court to another, where many people came to tell lies about Him. Jesus had not done anything wrong. The courts did not know what to do with Jesus, since He had done nothing wrong. Instead of releasing Him, they sent Jesus to be beaten before sending Him to the next court. Finally, they sent Him to Pontius Pilate. Pilate was the Roman governor in charge of Jerusalem.

Pilate knew Jesus had done nothing wrong, but a mob of people were outside yelling for Pilate to crucify Jesus. Pilate offered to release Jesus, but the mob decided they would rather Pilate release a dangerous criminal. Pilate sent Jesus to be beaten, hoping that after He was beaten, the mob would go away. But the crowd started chanting, "Crucify Him! Crucify Him!" Finally, Pilate sentenced Jesus to death on the cross. Jesus was crucified between two criminals. One of the criminals started to make fun of Jesus, but the other criminal knew Jesus was not a criminal.

Read Luke 23:40-43.

Jesus forgave the thief while He was dying on the cross. Can you believe that? But Jesus came to earth to take the punishment for our sins. He came so you and I can be forgiven for our sins and have a new relationship, a friendship, with God.

Jesus died and was buried in a tomb. Then three days later, He came back to life! That is the best news anyone has ever received! Jesus is not just a good guy who taught some good things about God. Jesus is not just a prophet who heard from God. Jesus IS God! And Jesus is ALIVE today! He is RISEN!!

 # APPLICATION

Jesus' sacrifice for us and resurrection three days later is the best news the world has EVER received. Because Jesus died and came back to life, we can have a friendship with God. Because Jesus died and rose again, we don't have to be afraid of anything. Jesus is our Friend. We can be part of the family of God.

And although most of us remember in our heads Jesus paid the punishment for our sins, we sometimes forget in our hearts how important that fact is. We start to think maybe our wrong choices aren't that important. "After all, everyone makes fun of that teacher. If I don't get caught, it doesn't really matter, right?"

But the truth is, it does matter. It matters so much Jesus, the Son of God, came from Heaven to earth, so we could be right with God again. So this Easter season, let's not let everything else around us cloud our memory of Jesus. Let's remember how much Jesus loves us and wants to have a friendship with us. Remember how much our sin cost. Remember how amazing it is that we serve a God who would sacrifice so much just to be close to us. Let's remember Jesus' sacrifice - not just in our heads, but in our hearts, too.

PRAY

OFFERING SONG

Lead the congregation in a slower worship song.

JUMP SKIT PART 2

See skit script beginning on page 149.

REMEMBER JESUS' SACRIFICE.

JUMP NEWS

REMEMBER JESUS' SACRIFICE.

Skit Intro Video

Welcome to JUMP NEWS with your news team: Weather with Wendy Storm, Traffic with Iona Ford, Sports with Will Wynn, Politics with Cam Pain, and news anchors, Justin Report and Johnny Onthespot.

SFX: NEWS TRANSITION MUSIC

JAMIE: Welcome back to JUMP NEWS, I'm Jamie Jamison.

Producer holds up "Applause" sign.

JAMIE: We are back with live coverage right outside of Police Chief Manor, the home of our beloved Police Chief of Hock-A-Mookie Falls. That's right viewers at home, our town has been so selflessly served and protected by this man, the City Council officially named his house after his distinguished position on the force. We now go live on site for our exclusive coverage of the Last Dinner and speech from our very own Police Chief, Hector Ulysses Goneoutski. *Scoop starts to laugh.* Tell us how things are going there, Scoop.

Lights up on Scoop standing next to a "Congratulations" sign.

SCOOP: *Laughing harder and harder.* That is crazy! Haha!

Producer, confused, holds up "Laugh" sign.

JAMIE: *Forced laugh.* Haha! What's so funny, Scoop?

SCOOP: Goneoutski? Ha! I never knew that was the Police Chief's name. Hahaha!

JAMIE: Well, it is his name, and I don't see what is so funny about it.

SCOOP: *Still laughing.* Are you kidding me? That name is hilarious. Hector Ulysses Goneoutski?! His initials spell ... HUG! *Bursts out laughing again.*

Producer, still confused, holds up "Laugh" sign.

SCOOP: If you are the Police Chief, you can't just go around hugging everyone. *Laughing even harder.*

JAMIE: *Shaking his head.* I really don't think the Police Chief that has served our town for 33 years has just gone around hugging everyone.

SCOOP: *Still laughing.* I would really hope not. Can you imagine someone trying to rob the bank and the Police Chief shows up at the crime scene and is like … *Acting it out.* "Hey bad guys, come over here and stop trying to rob our bank and give me a hug."

JAMIE: Well, that is completely ridiculous!

SCOOP: *Still laughing.* That's what I'm saying!

JAMIE: Well Scoop, thank you for that. Strange look into what your mind is doing at any given moment. However, can we now get back to the coverage of the Last Dinner?

SCOOP: Ah yes. Right! I'm Scoop Blakely, here to give you the scoop. We are now reporting live right outside of Police Chief Manor where once we go inside, we will hear the final speech from our Police Chief. This is a man who has been an incredible leader, and tonight we honor him by looking back at all of the amazing guidance, incredible bravery.

Producer hold up "Applause" sign.

SCOOP: And, of course, his warm hugs. Hahaha! I'm just kidding! Let's head inside.

As Scoop heads "inside" the party that has been going on the entire scene, we cut back to Jamie in the studio to allow transitional time for the set up on the other side of the stage.

JAMIE: Thank you, Scoop. When we come back we will be inside Police Chief Manor. See you in a moment!

Video: Commercial

PRODUCER: And we're live in 3, 2, 1 ….

JAMIE: And we are back. Let's go live on site with our temporary news anchor Scoop. *Jamie waits for Scoop to begin speaking, but Scoop just stands there waiting for the cue.* Scoop? Still Nothing. We are going live to you, Scoop.

SCOOP: *After a few seconds of a blank stare, Scoop, who is now inside the party, begins speaking loudly.* Thank you, Jamie, glad you guys went to commercial when you did, because I tripped over one of the guests in here and fell onto an entire plate of shrimp. One got stuck in my ear, and I'm pretty sure it has ruined my ear piece and is affecting my hearing. I couldn't hear you at all.

JAMIE: That is extremely gross, and I just can't imagine how you could have possibly …

SCOOP: *Interrupting.* Well, since I can't hear you, I will just direct your attention to the Police Chief who is about to make his final remarks.

POLICE CHIEF: Citizens of the great city of Hock-A-Mookie Falls, both gathered here and watching at home, I am so honored to be recognized tonight by all of you. *Lifting up speech that has been written down.* I would like to read to you the remainder of my speech so I make sure to say all of the things I would like for you to hear tonight. *Begins reading.* It is true I have sacrificed many things in this 33 years of service. The truth is, however, when we all, any of us, walk down the street and experience the freedom we get to enjoy by choosing to live inside of the law of this fantastic town, the sacrifices seem small and unimportant. It has been the greatest privilege of my life to lead and guide this fair city, and as I leave from this great office, I want you to think about, and remember, the things that we have all learned. We have learned how to live, what to do, what not to do, and how to not only know these things in our heads, but act on them with our lives. You see, great people of Hock-A-Mookie Falls, the reason this town is great, is not because all of us know what to do, it is because most of us here know Jesus. When we choose to remember Jesus in our hearts, we do what is right out of our love from Him. Continue to be great citizens. Continue to enjoy the great city of Hock-A-Mookie, and … *Pointing at Scoop.* Continue to try not to get shrimp stuck in your ear.

Producer hold up "Applause" sign. Everyone bursts into applause.

SCOOP: *Turning back to camera and speaking in his normal voice.* You have heard it here first on JUMP NEWS, ladies and gentlemen. Continue to remember the great sacrifice the Police Chief made for our great town by not only knowing what to do in your head, but by letting your knowledge of right and wrong change the way you live with and toward others. Continue to remember Jesus' ultimate sacrifice, as we obey Him out of our love for Him. And most importantly, don't go to any fancy dinner parties, trip and get shrimp stuck in your ear. That's all for now. This is Scoop signing off with JUMP NEWS live on location at Police Chief Manor. Back to you, Jamie.

JAMIE: Surprisingly, job well done, Scoop! Thanks for the ... Well, scoop, Scoop! That's all we have for you tonight, folks. Please join us next time when we have special guest artist Rockadilly Rhonda and her Yodeling Band of Wild Jungle Gophers. *Squints at the teleprompter.* Really? Is that right? Yodeling Band of Wild Jungle Gophers? *Looking around for confirmation.* This has been JUMP NEWS with Jamie Jamison and Scoop Blakely. Remember, when life hands you lemons, check for mold.

SFX: NEWS TRANSITION MUSIC

SONG *Lead the congregation in a fun worship song.*

MEMORY VERSE VIDEO

MEMORY VERSE

Our memory verse is from the book of Luke, chapter four, verses eighteen and nineteen. These verses are about Jesus!

Read the verses with me. **Luke 4:18-19 "The Spirit of the LORD is upon me, for he has anointed me to bring Good News to the poor. He has sent me to proclaim that captives will be released, that the blind will see, that the oppressed will be set free, and that the time of the LORD's favor has come."**

The Good News is that Jesus made a way for us to have a right relationship with God. I'm glad God loves us so much He sent His Son, Jesus, to take the punishment for our sins. Because of Jesus, we can be a part of God's forever family. Jesus is the best news the world has ever received! Let's review the motions to what we have learned so far.

Repeat after me.
Luke 4:18-19 (*Luke 4:18-19*)
"The Spirit of the LORD is upon me (*The Spirit of the LORD is upon me*),
for he has anointed me to bring (*for he has anointed me to bring*)
Good News to the poor (*Good News to the poor*).
He has sent me to proclaim (*He has sent me to proclaim*)
that captives will be released (*that captives will be released*),
that the blind will see (*that the blind will see*)
that the oppressed will be set free (*that the oppressed will be set free*)
and that the time of the LORD's favor (*and that the time of the LORD's favor*)
has come (*has come*)."

Jesus is God's promised Savior. He came from heaven to earth to take our punishment for our sins, our wrong choices. Jesus loves us so much! When we choose to believe in Him, to make Him the Boss of our lives, Jesus will change our hearts forever. That is Good News!

Stand up and let's say both verses together, starting with "Luke 4:18-19" on the count of three. One, two, three: **Luke 4:18-19 "The Spirit of the LORD is upon me, for he has anointed me to bring Good News to the poor. He has sent me to proclaim that captives will be released, that the blind will see, that the oppressed will be set free, and that the time of the LORD's favor has come."**

We have worked very hard to memorize these verses. Can you say the verses without my help and without looking at the screens? Remember, we start with "Luke 4:18-19."

Take the verse off the screens. If you are able, video your congregation reciting the verses from memory. Show the video in your next session.

One, two, three: **Luke 4:18-19 "The Spirit of the LORD is upon me, for he has anointed me to bring Good News to the poor. He has sent me to proclaim that captives will be released, that the blind will see, that the oppressed will be set free, and that the time of the LORD's favor has come."**

You are amazing! I am so proud of you. Remember, Jesus is the best news the world has ever received! I challenge you to tell someone the Good News about Jesus this week.

ANNOUNCEMENTS

Use this time to encourage kids to bring friends and participate in whatever you may have coming up next.

REVIEW GAME

It's time for the REVIEW GAME!! I need one volunteer from each grade to come up on stage. I will choose people who have been listening and paying attention the whole service and want to play in our game.

Choose contestants and introduce them to the group in game show style.

During this game, your grade can win by getting very quiet when you hear the wrong answer and very loud when you hear the right answer. Each grade is going to have a different silly move and sound that you must do when you think you hear the right answer. (*Let your contestants choose a silly motion and sound for their grade.*)

I hope you are ready. I hope you have been paying attention, because the game begins ... NOW!

Give kids the opportunity to do their motions and silly sounds when they hear the correct answer. Award points to the grade who is the quietest when they hear the wrong answer and participates the most when they hear the right answer.

Question 1: What was today's Main Point?
    a. Remember to Clean Your Room.
    b. Remember to Take Out the Trash.
    c. Remember Jesus' Sacrifice.
    d. When Life Hands You Lemons, Check for Mold.

Question 2: Where can you find today's Bible lesson?
    a. Luke 22-24
    b. Judas 22-24
    c. Leviticus 22-24
    d. Luke 2

Question 3: At the Last Supper, what represented Jesus' body?
    a. broken spaghetti
    b. crushed candy
    c. broken bread
    d. chicken

For added fun, play "The Chicken Dance" each time you read a wrong answer about chickens. Act bewildered, like you do not know where the music is coming from. Read the question again and continue.

Question 4: At the Last Supper, what represented Jesus' blood?
    a. wine
    b. water
    c. broken bread
    d. chicken

Question 5: How did Jesus show His great love for us?
    a. He cooked a nice meal.
    b. He died on the cross for our sins and came back to life three days later.
    c. He sang a beautiful song.
    d. He did the chicken dance.

Question 6: Luke 4:18-19 says, "He has sent me to proclaim that captives will be released, that the blind will see, that the oppressed will be set free, and that the time of the _____ _____ has come."
    a. remembering this verse
    b. dancing fever
    c. LORD's favor
    d. Taco Tuesday

SONG

Lead the congregation in a fun worship song.

DISMISSAL

NOTES

NOTES

NOTES

nineteen

™

KIDS

Reaching kids and their families for Christ
by making programming for children
Fun, Intentional, Scriptural, and Helpful.

I've never seen a curriculum that is both scripturally
sound AND as fun as VBS! You've got to try it!

Karen M. | Children's Curriculum Developer

· · · · · · · · **"** · · · · · · · ·

28nineteen™ can work with any church -
whatever their size or their schedule.

Elizabeth W. | Children's Ministry Professional

www.28nineteencurriculum.com